AMERICAN HERITAGE

BATTLE MAPS
of the
CIVIL WAR

*General Grant with
staff members viewing a map.*

AMERICAN HERITAGE

BATTLE MAPS
of the
CIVIL WAR

Text by
Richard O'Shea

Featuring Maps by
David Greenspan

Introduction by
Robert K. Krick

Council Oak Books
Tulsa

This 1992 edition is published by
COUNCIL OAK BOOKS
1350 East 15th Street
Tulsa, Oklahoma 74120
Tel: 800-247-8850
Fax: 918-583-4995

Produced by Freundlich Associates, Inc.
333 East 30th Street
New York, NY 10016
Design and production: Anthony Meisel Publishing Services
Origination and printing: Regent Publishing Services Ltd.

Printed in Singapore

ISBN 0-933031-71-8

CONTENTS

Council of War *by Don Stivers. Lee and his generals review tactics before Gettysburg.*

INTRODUCTION

The writer Robert Louis Stevenson once remarked, "I am told that there are people who do not care for maps, and I find it hard to believe." The great Scottish literary figure referred not to the maps necessary for an understanding of military affairs but, rather, to those required for the quotidian transactions of human existence. Any serious reader of military history will instantly recognize and redouble Stevenson's astonishment that anyone could be indifferent to maps. Even so, major accumulations of Civil War tactical maps are remarkably scarce. Good books about the war contain good and plentiful maps on their specific subjects; bad books contain few or none. This book is about maps and is full of maps and related illustrations covering the entire war. Its advent will serve students of the war admirably well.

The men who fought the American Civil War labored under the daunting disadvantage of attempting to move huge armies across rough terrain without adequate knowledge of the ground. Maps available to army commanders often were poor, sometimes even dreadful. One of the amazing aspects of Robert E. Lee's first campaign with the Army of Northern Virginia is that throughout the Seven Days' battles—though in the presumably familiar outskirts of his country's capital city—he commanded without the benefit of accurate maps. Nearly one year later, Stonewall Jackson successfully completed his spectacular flank march and attack at Chancellorsville on the basis of a tiny pencil-scribbled map of astonishing simplicity.

In studying Civil War engagements, we are fortunate to have good maps and charts at hand, but it is appropriate to bear firmly in mind the artificial advantage that comes from the superior understanding that we can synthesize with hindsight. A detailed tactical history of the Battle of Cedar Mountain that I wrote includes sixteen maps. Again and again, in speaking to groups about the battle or touring them over the ground, I have watched individuals, with the maps in front of them, unravel tactical quandaries and then ask why on earth one general or another did not behave differently. That sort of thoughtful analysis is both stimulating and legitimate, but it must be accompanied by a clear recognition that military history turns chaos into order as a means of understanding. That understanding must then have a sense of chaos reimposed upon it, to avoid an unreasonable assumption of omnipotence. In using the excellent materials in this book, and military maps in general, observe the caveat of A. P. Wavell:

"Remember that war is always a far worse muddle than anything you can produce in peace."

It is instructive, though hardly surprising, to note that some famous figures of the Civil War era acquired their prominence by wielding mapping gear rather than military equipage. Jedediah Hotchkiss is more familiar to the average Civil War enthusiast than are at least two-thirds of the Confederates who rose to general officer rank. Hotchkiss's role as mapmaker for Jackson, though he held no military rank whatsoever under that general and saw very little fighting, keeps him firmly fixed in our minds. Without deprecating the military service of Federals Nathaniel Michler and Ezra A. Carman, we can recognize that both men are memorable and important because of their mapping pens, not their swords. Jed Hotchkiss also earned deserved attention as co-author of two volumes of postwar military history (about Chancellorsville and the Shenandoah Valley Campaign), in conjunction with the brilliant William Allan of Jackson's staff. Once again, maps supplied a cachet for Hotchkiss, because he apparently contributed little or nothing to the written narrative of either book.

Military histories of the war written over the century and a quarter since its conclusion often stand or fall on the strength of the maps they offer to readers. John Bigelow's massive and masterful *The Campaign of Chancellorsville* (New Haven: Yale University Press, 1910) has been called, with some merit, the best study of any American campaign from any American war. Bigelow's examination of Chancellorsville is careful and thorough, if focused by design primarily on Union operations. It certainly would deserve accolades even without the vast array of multicolored maps that accompany the text. Without those maps, however, no one would think of Bigelow when contemplating a "best ever" listing.

The crucial relationship of maps to Civil War military history is vividly illustrated by a series of battle studies published on the eve of the Civil War centennial. The series included hardbound books on most of the major campaigns in the eastern theater by a single author. The narratives offered little or nothing to a serious historian, and at times foisted frightful gaffes on an unsuspecting general readership. Even the most dedicated students of the war eagerly bought the books nonetheless, and knowledgeable collectors still do, because each volume contains numerous maps drawn by a skilled historian hired by the author.

In the same vein, the two standard histories of the Battle of Antietam appeal for different reasons. A fine recent narrative, supported by admirable research, features maps not so good as those of an earlier book that is not as strong in research and writing.

Maps are mandatory companions to the study of Civil War history in part because terrain affects military affairs so markedly. It is a truism that geographical imperatives channel the flow of most human history in important ways, but in military matters the terrain factor looms larger than ever. In an apt line, General Nathanael Greene in 1781 declared: "The British may harass us and distress us, but the Carolinas alone can subdue us." At the tactical level, one of Baron Henri Jomini's nineteenth-century maxims is apposite: "There is in every battlefield a decisive point the possession of which, more than any other, helps to secure victory by enabling its holder to make a proper application of the principles of war." Jomini's decisive point at First Manassas was Henry House Hill; at Cedar Mountain it was the eponymous mountain itself; at Fredericksburg it was Marye's Heights; at Chancellorsville it was Hazel Grove; at Wilderness it was the Brock Road–Plank Road intersection. Discerning those points of decision and control, on maps crude at best, won battles for Civil War leaders. Failure to do so lost battles for other leaders. Identifying the deadly landmarks and understanding them are readily achievable for 1990s students of the war, so long as good maps are at hand. This book offers a major step in that direction.

The World War II generation of military professionals had an axiom that will strike a sympathetic response among students of battles: "Battle is a process which always takes place at the junction of two maps." The Civil War corollary of this Military Murphy's Law is that every engagement of the 1860s took place in the crease of at least two, and probably three or even four, quadrangles of the modern U.S.G.S. topographic maps. The uncanny knack with which that result occurs has prompted some cynics to suggest that the mappers used the battlefields as benchmarks in laying out grid corners (rather like the way the Virginia Department of Highways seems to seek out battlefields in routing major highways). Modern technology supplies a ready means to achieve the sweeping *coup d'oeil* denied by fragmentary map segments; aerial photography provides a comprehensive picture that obviously was unavailable to the participants but can be an important aid to our understanding. This volume offers that aerial perspective as a welcome addition to our historical tools as we set out to examine the battlefields.

Maps are a simple necessity for any study of the Civil War. This book full of maps, combined with revealing aerial photographs and impressively offset by Troiani art, will be a useful companion for anyone reading of the war.

Robert K. Krick
Fredericksburg, Virginia
April 1992

PREFACE

The very first book that triggered my enduring passion for the American Civil War was *A History of the Civil War* by Benson Lossing, published in 1912. It contained Mathew Brady photographs and color illustrations by H. A. Ogden, depicting military officers, standing or on horseback, overlooking dramatic battle scenes. The impact that book had on me was enormous, and although I did not read Mr. Lossing's plodding text with true diligence, the black-and-white photographs and the art work touched off in me a hunger for books on the Civil War that has not abated in forty-seven years.

Another major book influence was a four–volume set by John Codman Ropes and W. R. Livermore, *The Story of the Civil War*, published between 1894–1913. It had a splendid set of separate maps in a pouch in the back, which gave me my first exposure to the use of maps that showed what happened, where everyone went, and what they did when they got there. It was quickly apparent that good maps were going to be my key to the enjoyment of Civil War campaigns and battles. Unfortunately, the problem with most maps that appear in Civil War books today, if they appear at all, is that generally you need to refer to them over several pages of text, so you must back-page to a map while awkwardly holding it in place with your finger.

Over the years, there have been several atlases and books published that feature maps of the great battles and campaigns of the Civil War. For the most part, these books are quite handsomely done. The trouble is that they vary in their degree of clarity and portability. As an example, I mention *The Official Military Atlas of the Civil War* printed by the National Historical Society in 1978. The problem for the average reader is that the book weighs nine pounds, and measures more than a foot by a foot and a third.

The purpose of this book is to utilize the clarity and compactness of a series of maps created by David Greenspan in 1951, at the request of American Heritage. When I first realized the need for clear maps and views of Civil War battle movements, I began to clip battle maps and bird's–eye depictions from various books and magazines. These I collected in a special binder for my personal reference. I found myself buying old and worn copies of books so that my clippings would not damage my own good copy of the same book.

Premier within my collection were the Greenspan maps, because they were virtually unmatched for the type of image they created. These served to place you just above the action, as if in an observation balloon. Sacrificed in these overviews, however, was an exactness of distance and detail—such as the precise number of houses or buildings in and around the field of battle or line of march. For the purist, however, these abandoned details could be compensated for by reference to the more traditional two–dimensional, tactical maps with arrows and boxes. That special binder full of maps was the prototype for this book. I remind the purist that not every major battle is covered here by Mr. Greenspan's artistry. By the same measure, the introductory text to my chapters is lean and it is intended not to provide a multilayered analysis of the war but, rather, to bridge you from each grouping of maps to the next, providing you with a map-driven narrative of the great battles and campaigns of the Civil War.

Richard O'Shea

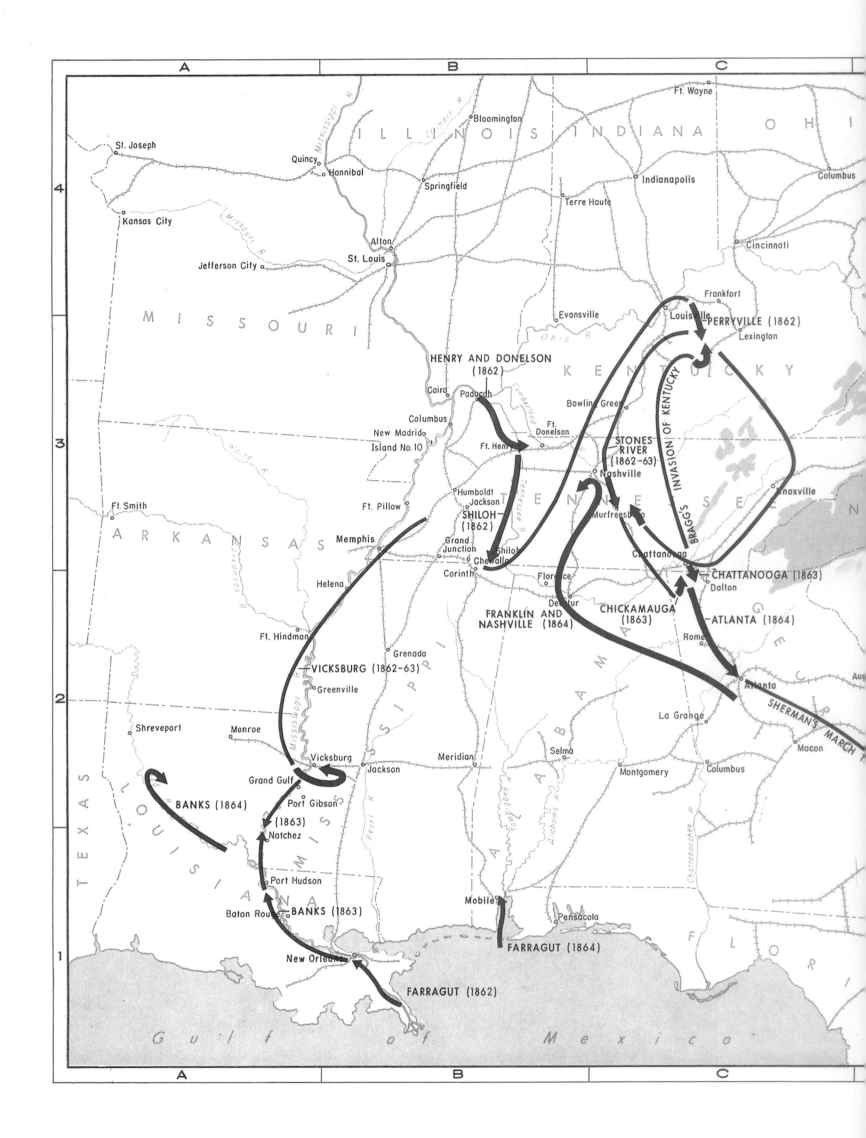

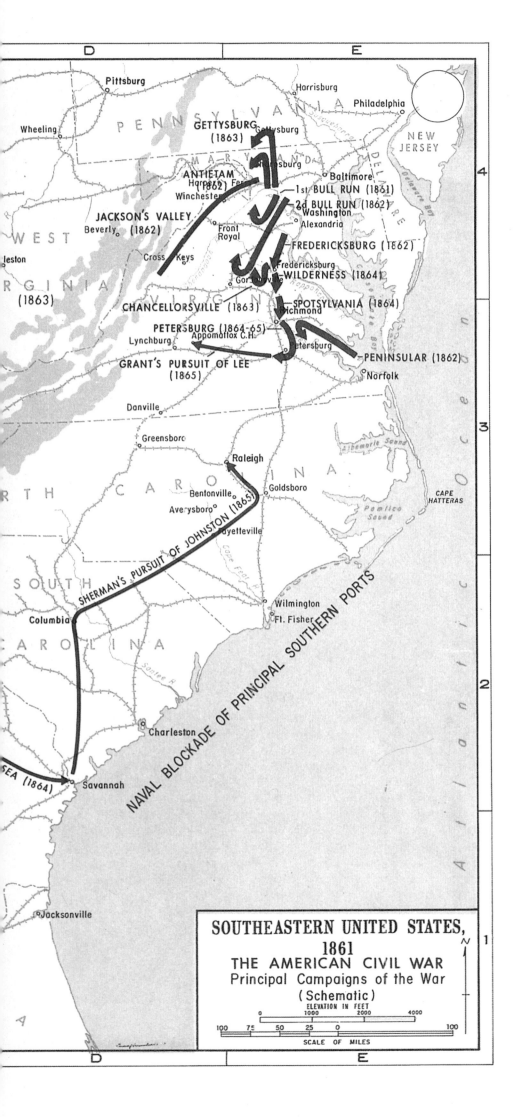

TABLE OF SYMBOLS

BASIC SYMBOLS

Regiment		Infantry
Brigade		Cavalry
Division		Cavalry Covering Force
Corps		Artillery
Army		Artillery In Position
		(Does not indicate type or quantity)
		Trains

EXAMPLES OF COMBINATIONS OF BASIC SYMBOLS

Barksdale's Infantry Brigade
of McLaws' Division
Barksdale (McLaws)

Stuart's Cavalry Division
Minus Detachments
Stuart (–)

First Corps

Rosecrans' Army
of the Cumberland
CUMBERLAND ROSECRANS

OTHER SYMBOLS

	Actual location	Prior location		
Troops on the march			Troops displacing and direction	
Troops in position			Troops in position under attack	
Troops in bivouac or reserve			Route of march	
			Strong prepared positions	
			Battle Sites	

Map labels:

PENNSYLVANIA

Pittsburg
Harrisburg
Philadelphia
Wheeling
NEW JERSEY
GETTYSBURG (1863)
Gettysburg
MARYLAND
Baltimore
ANTIETAM (1862)
Harpers Ferry
Winchester
1st BULL RUN (1861)
2d BULL RUN (1862)
Washington
Alexandria
JACKSON'S VALLEY (1862)
Beverly
Front Royal
FREDERICKSBURG (1862)
WEST VIRGINIA (1863)
Cross Keys
Fredericksburg
WILDERNESS (1864)
Gordonsville
SPOTSYLVANIA (1864)
CHANCELLORSVILLE (1863)
Richmond
PETERSBURG (1864-65)
Appomattox C.H.
Lynchburg
Petersburg
PENINSULAR (1862)
GRANT'S PURSUIT OF LEE (1865)
Norfolk
Danville
Greensboro
Raleigh
NORTH CAROLINA
Bentonville
Goldsboro
CAPE HATTERAS
Averysboro
Pamlico Sound
Albemarle Sound
Fayetteville
Cape Fear
SHERMAN'S PURSUIT OF JOHNSTON (1865)
Wilmington
Ft. Fisher
NAVAL BLOCKADE OF PRINCIPAL SOUTHERN PORTS
SOUTH CAROLINA
Columbia
Charleston
Santee R
Savannah
SEA (1864)
Jacksonville
Atlantic Ocean
Chesapeake Bay
Delaware Bay

SOUTHEASTERN UNITED STATES, 1861
THE AMERICAN CIVIL WAR
Principal Campaigns of the War
(Schematic)

ELEVATION IN FEET
1000   2000   4000

100   75   50   25   0   100
SCALE OF MILES

The Balance Sheet as War Began

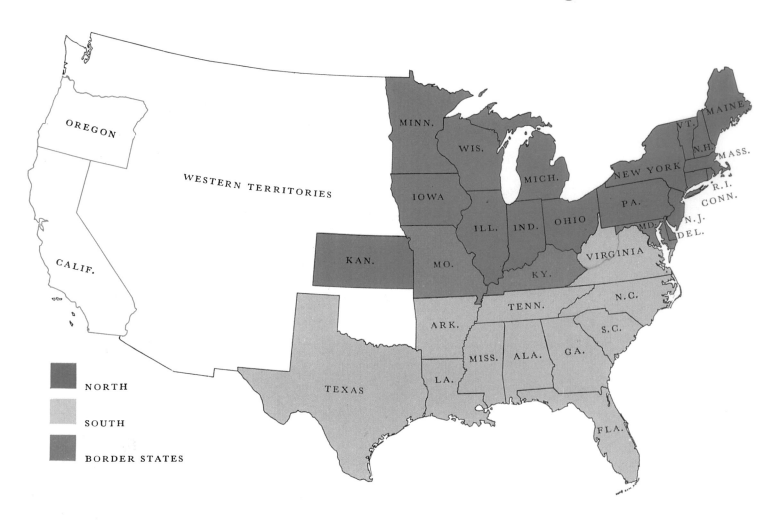

NORTH

SOUTH

BORDER STATES

The 34-star, prewar flag of 1861 symbolized an expanding Union. In the last decade the nation had leapfrogged over the prairies and mountains to admit California and Oregon; on the eve of Lincoln's inauguration Kansas came into the fold. Moreover, the Eighth Census, taken in 1860, revealed a country expanding in directions other than geographical. It showed a population increasing in almost geometric progression, a healthy agricultural boom, and an industry bursting at the seams. But a careful study of these statistics discloses a remarkable disproportion between the nation's two major sections—North and South.

In area there was little difference. The square mileage of eighteen Northern states (minus California and Oregon, which were too far distant to contribute much more than moral support to the coming conflict) was actually surpassed by the eleven Confederate states. Three brittle border states—Kentucky, Maryland, and Missouri—might swing either way; and, for this reason, they are shown in the graphs on the opposite page as a separate category.

In population (Graph 1) the North was double the size of the South, whose population was nearly 40 per cent slave. Of six leading agricultural products (Graph 2) the South led in three; but of these, only one was an edible crop. The scales were not so heavily weighted in favor of the North in the livestock category (Graph 3).

Railroad mileage (Graph 4) must be interpreted in terms of total territory—the North had more than twice the mileage of the South for an almost equal area. The statistics for manufacturing and finance (Graphs 5 and 6) expose the basic shortcomings of an agricultural South in an industrial age.

This balance sheet of assets on the eve of war reveals a disparity that was far from apparent at the time to the two hostile factions.

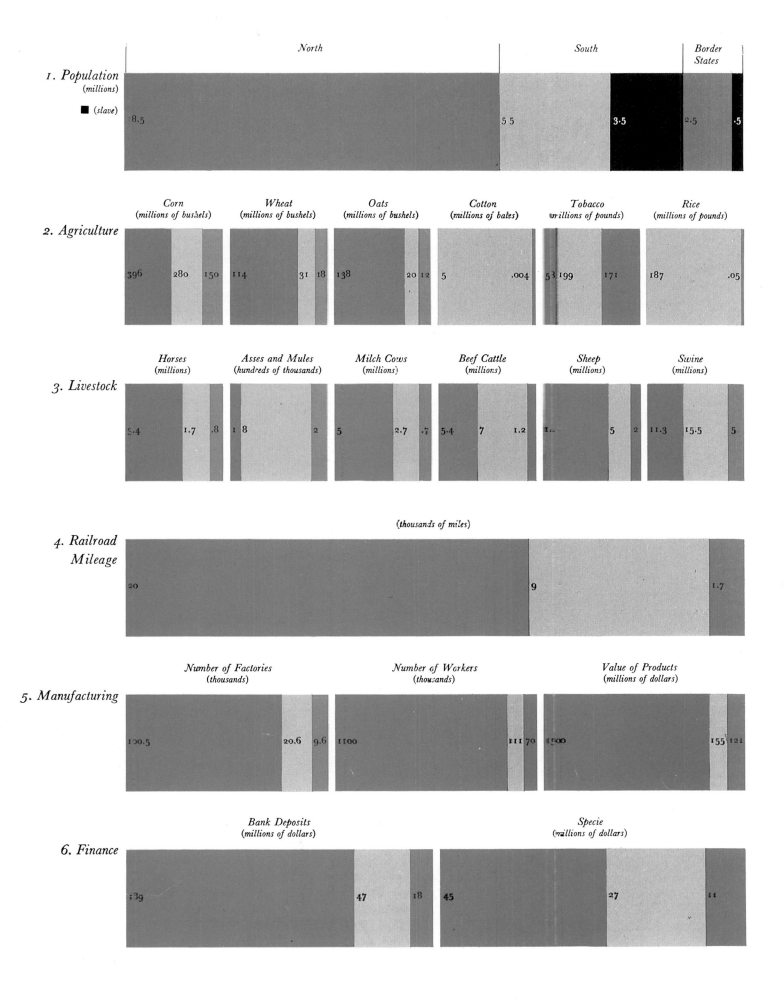

1. Population
(millions)

■ (slave)

North — 18.5

South — 5.5 | 3.5

Border States — 2.5 | .5

2. Agriculture

Corn (millions of bushels)	Wheat (millions of bushels)	Oats (millions of bushels)	Cotton (millions of bales)	Tobacco (millions of pounds)	Rice (millions of pounds)
396 · 280 · 150	114 · 31 · 18	138 · 20 · 12	5 · .004	53 · 199 · 171	187 · .05

3. Livestock

Horses (millions)	Asses and Mules (hundreds of thousands)	Milch Cows (millions)	Beef Cattle (millions)	Sheep (millions)	Swine (millions)
3.4 · 1.7 · .8	1 · 8 · 2	5 · 2.7 · .7	5.4 · 7 · 1.2	14 · 5 · 2	11.3 · 15.5 · 5

4. Railroad Mileage
(thousands of miles)

20 · 9 · 1.7

5. Manufacturing

Number of Factories (thousands)	Number of Workers (thousands)	Value of Products (millions of dollars)
100.5 · 20.6 · 9.6	1100 · 111 · 70	1500 · 155 · 121

6. Finance

Bank Deposits (millions of dollars)	Specie (millions of dollars)
189 · 47 · 18	45 · 27 · 11

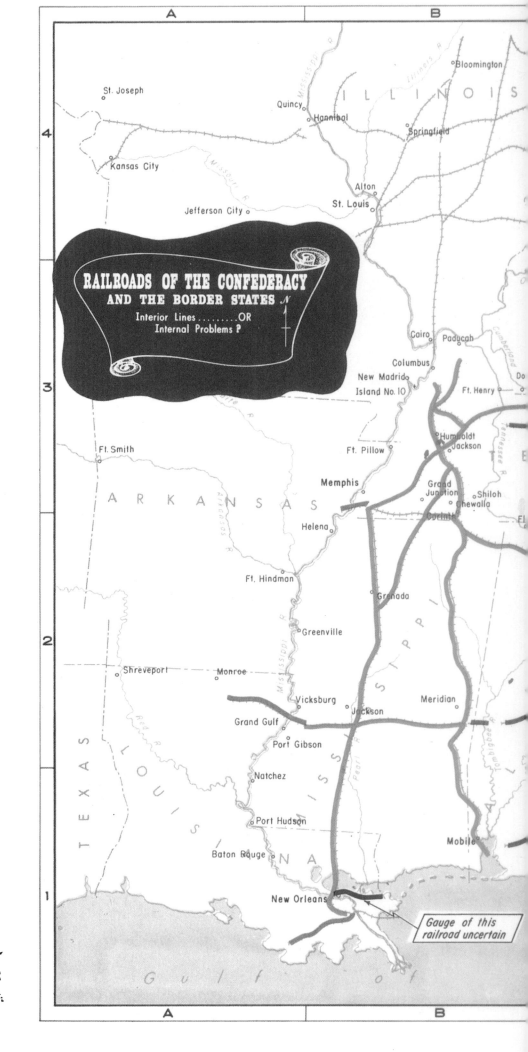

RAILROADS OF THE CONFEDERACY
AND THE BORDER STATES N

Interior Lines.........OR
Internal Problems?

Gauge of this railroad uncertain

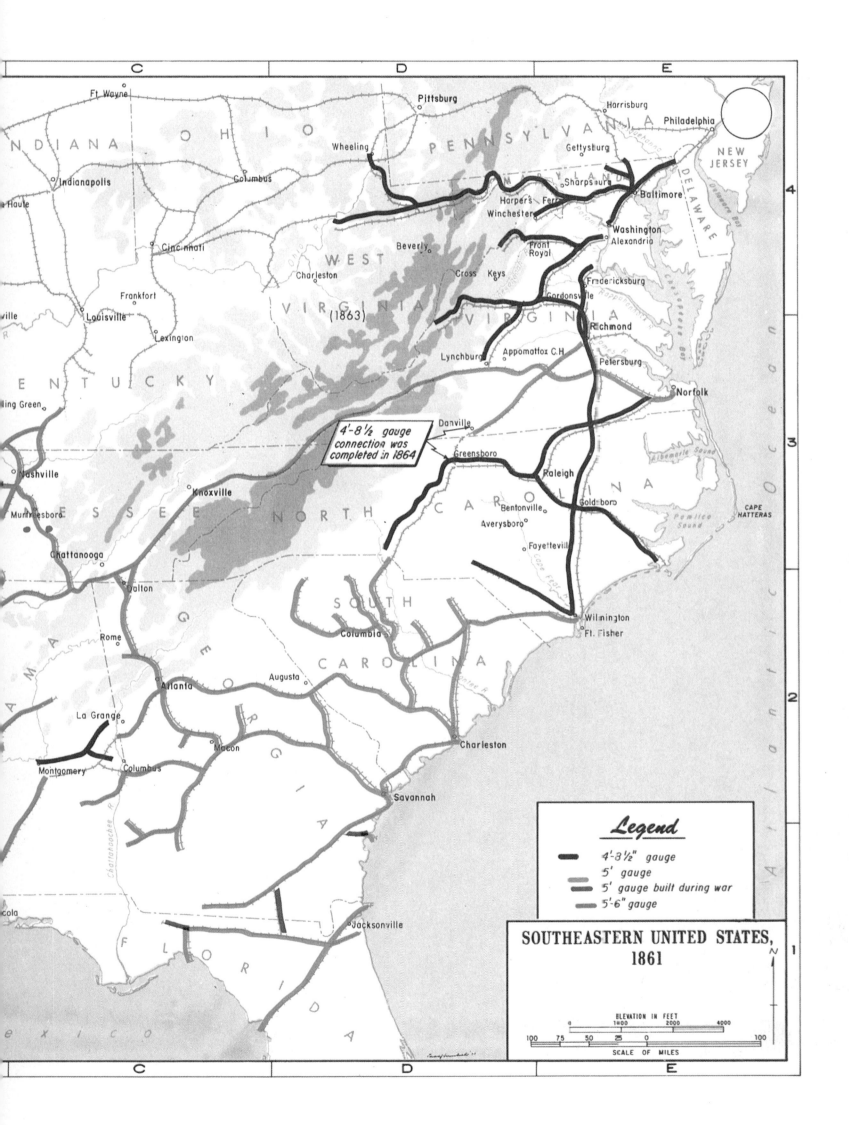

4'-8½ gauge connection was completed in 1864

Legend

▬▬ 4'-8½" gauge
▬▬ 5' gauge
▬▬ 5' gauge built during war
▬▬ 5'-6" gauge

SOUTHEASTERN UNITED STATES, 1861

ELEVATION IN FEET

SCALE OF MILES

20105355

THE FIRST BATTLE OF BULL RUN
(First Manassas)

July 21, 1861

Following the attack on Fort Sumter on April 12, 1861, President Abraham Lincoln called for 75,000 volunteers to fight against the seceding states. The secession of Virginia and North Carolina followed rapidly, and in June the Confederacy moved its capital from Montgomery, Alabama, to Richmond, Virginia. With the Northern and Southern capitals separated by only one hundred miles, Virginia was to become a major battleground.

Both sides set to work creating armies. Many of the hastily gathered Confederate militias had been selected from organizations that, before the war, had been strictly social groups. Troops on both sides were erratically equipped and erratically uniformed. The regular Union army had been built from only 16,000 men, drawn from all parts of the country.

Most regular United States Army officers of Southern origin resigned their commissions and returned home to fight against their former comrades. Neither side was prepared for what was to follow.

The Confederate government, hoping to hold northern Virginia and menace Washington, D.C., occupied Manassas Junction, linking the Manassas Gap and Orange and Alexandria railroads. Manassas was a scant twenty miles from Washington, and before being driven off, Confederate outposts around Alexandria, Virginia, would find themselves with an excellent view of the Capitol and the surrounding buildings of the Union government.

On July 15, 20,000 Confederate troops, commanded by Pierre G. T. Beauregard, the "Hero of Sumter," were prepared for battle. Joseph E. Johnston, one of the most distinguished of the United States Army defectors to the Southern cause, commanded 12,000 troops near Winchester, Virginia. A small detachment of 3,000 men, under Theophilus Holmes, occupied the strategic landing at Aquia Creek, near Fredericksburg, Virginia.

The Union had massed about 35,000 men near Washington, under the command of Irvin McDowell. A force of 18,000 Union soldiers, under Robert Patterson, pushed Johnston out of Harpers Ferry on June 15. It had crossed the Potomac River and was now camped around Charles Town, Virginia (now West Virginia). Johnston's objective was to hold Winchester in order to deny Union forces an entrance to the Shenandoah Valley.

The main Union thrust was to come from McDowell's army.

Patterson's job was to prevent Johnston's troops from coming to the aid of Beauregard, who, despite his smaller numbers, planned to defeat the Union army as it sallied forth from Washington. And with Northern newspaper headlines trumpeting "On to Richmond" and with considerable political pressure urging an attack, McDowell responded aggressively, though he took the field with inadequately equipped and poorly trained troops. Awaiting him at Manassas was an equally substandard force of the enemy.

McDowell began his march to Centreville, Virginia, on July 16, arriving there on July 18—a march of twenty miles in just over two days. The men were tired, and they lacked march discipline. Finally, however, they were concentrated in front of the enemy.

Meanwhile, Patterson seemed to have misunderstood his role of holding Johnston in place near Winchester. Patterson's orders had left him with too much discretion, and when he overestimated Johnston's strength, his concern over the safety of his supply lines led him to leave his advanced position at Bunker Hill, Virginia (now West Virginia), in order to withdraw toward

Above: Recent aerial view of the battlefield from 40,000 ft.
Dot: Henry House Hill. 1 incr = 1.26 miles.
Left: Railroad bridge over Bull Run after the battle.

FRANKLIN COUNTY LIBRARY
LOUISBURG, NC
BRANCHES IN BUNN,
FRANKLINTON & YOUNGSVILLE

Washington

Chantilly

Fairfax C.H.

CUB RUN

Centreville

CUB RUN
BRIDGE

⑨

BULL RUN

①

④

STONE
BRIDGE

ROBINSON
HOUSE

⑤

HENRY
HOUSE

HENRY HOUSE HILL

⑥

FIRST BULL RUN (or Manassas): A predawn Union feint is made at the Stone Bridge (1), as McDowell takes two divisions on a circuitous route to strike at Sudley Springs Ford (2). The Confederates are forced to swing their defense from Bull Run to Matthews Hill (3), where the day's first heavy fighting occurs. Colonel William T. Sherman moves his brigade across a ford (4) to strike at the new Rebel right, but the initial impetus of the Federal drive has been slowed. On the Henry House Hill the Southerners rally around T. J. Jackson's brigade (5). Union batteries near the Henry House hold their fire, and a Confederate regiment clothed in blue captures the position (6). Kirby Smith, leading the last of Johnston's troops to arrive at Manassas from the Shenandoah Valley, reaches the battlefield about 4 P.M.—in time to reinforce the Rebel line (7); and Jubal Early drives up from the southwest (8) to force a Union retirement. McDowell's withdrawal turns into a rout when an overturned wagon on Cub Run Bridge holds up the retreat (9). Afterward, the disorganized Union troops can scarcely be stopped short of Washington (in the distance at the upper right), some 25 miles away.

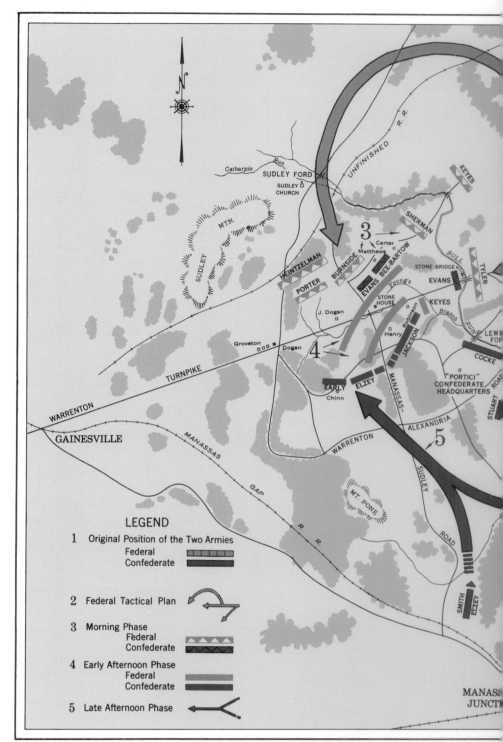

LEGEND

1   Original Position of the Two Armies
     Federal
     Confederate

2   Federal Tactical Plan

3   Morning Phase
     Federal
     Confederate

4   Early Afternoon Phase
     Federal
     Confederate

5   Late Afternoon Phase

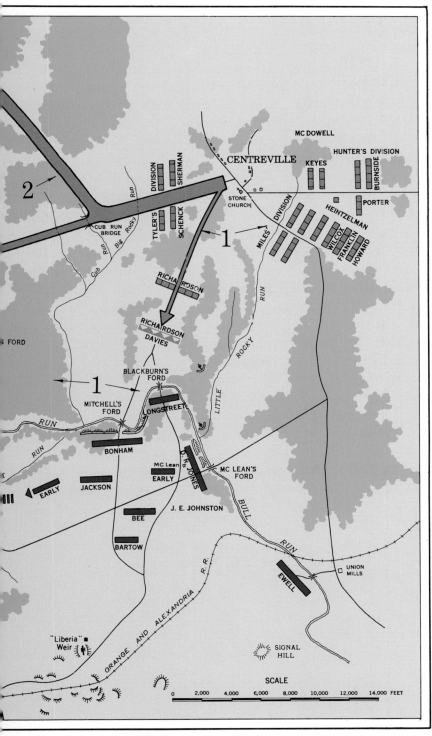

Harpers Ferry. This permitted Johnston, leaving Jeb Stuart's cavalry behind as a screen, to exercise his own discretionary orders and join Beauregard at Manassas.

Johnston began his advance on July 18. Beauregard had already sent Holmes's command en route to the battlefront and had placed his own brigades in a position well in advance of the important railhead at Manassas Junction. Beauregard's brigade was located along a narrow, muddy stream named Bull Run. Some of his brigadiers—Nathan G. Evans, Philip St. George Cocke, Milledge L. Bonham, and David R. Jones—remain largely unsung in Civil War annals; but three others—James Longstreet, Jubal Early, and Richard S. Ewell—were to become celebrated combat officers. Two of Johnston's four brigadiers, Francis Bartow and Barnard Bee, would die on the field at Manassas. The other two, Thomas J. (later "Stonewall") Jackson and Edmund Kirby Smith, would distinguish themselves in battles yet to be fought.

McDowell had organized his army into five divisions, commanded by Colonels David Hunter, Samuel P. Heintzelman, Daniel Tyler, Dixon S. Miles, and Theodore Runyon. McDowell's brigadiers included Erasmus Keyes, William T. Sherman, Israel Richardson, Oliver O. Howard, William B. Franklin, Fitz-John Porter, and Ambrose Burnside. On July 18, McDowell sent Tyler's division on a reconnaissance-in-force against the Confederate right the strongest part of Beauregard's line. This abortive attack convinced McDowell that his plan to turn the enemy's right flank was not workable, and he decided to attack the enemy's left.

McDowell planned to send Hunter and Heintzelman to cross upstream at Sudley Springs, thus cutting the Manassas Gap railway. In addition, Tyler and Richardson were to create diversionary flurries at Stone Bridge and Blackburn's Ford. By this time, however, cutting the railway had lost its purpose. Johnston's command, unknown to McDowell, had arrived on July 20, leaving only Kirby Smith's brigade still en route to the front. In the early morning of July 21 as McDowell's men moved out, they were to encounter an enemy of equal strength, one that not only had adequate reserves but also occupied an easily defensible position.

Left to right:
Maj. Gen. Irvin McDowell
Maj. Gen. William T. Sherman
Maj. Gen. Samuel P. Heintzelman
Gen. Joseph E. Johnston
Gen. Pierre G. T. Beauregard
Maj. Gen. Thomas J. Jackson

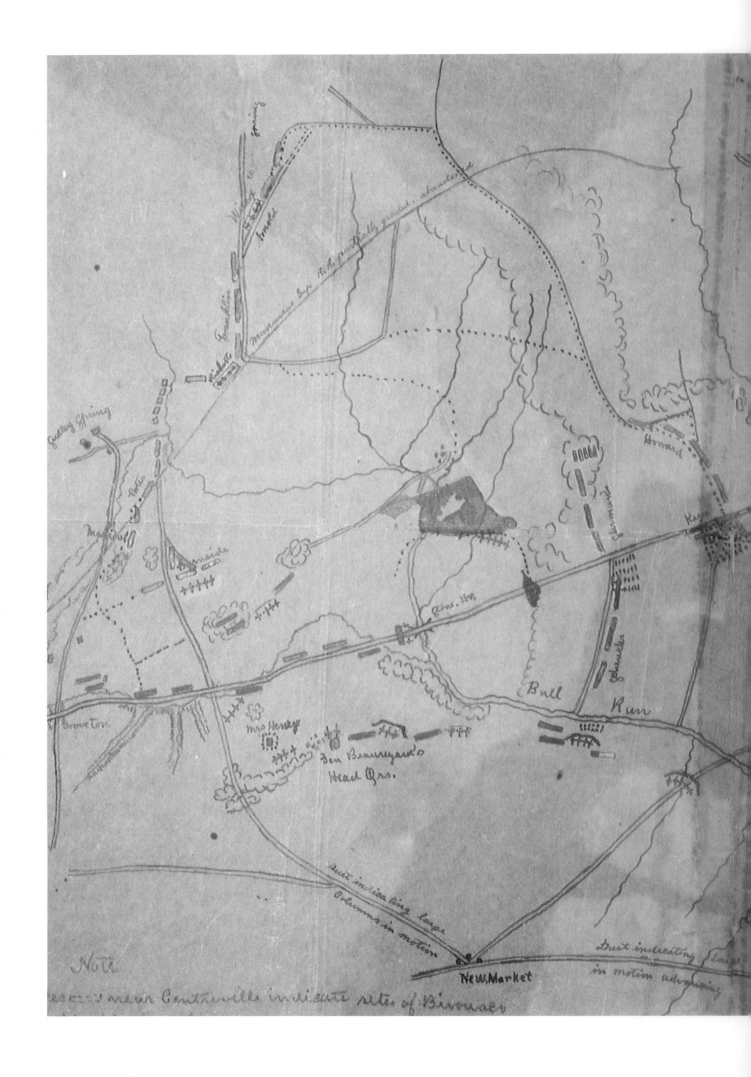

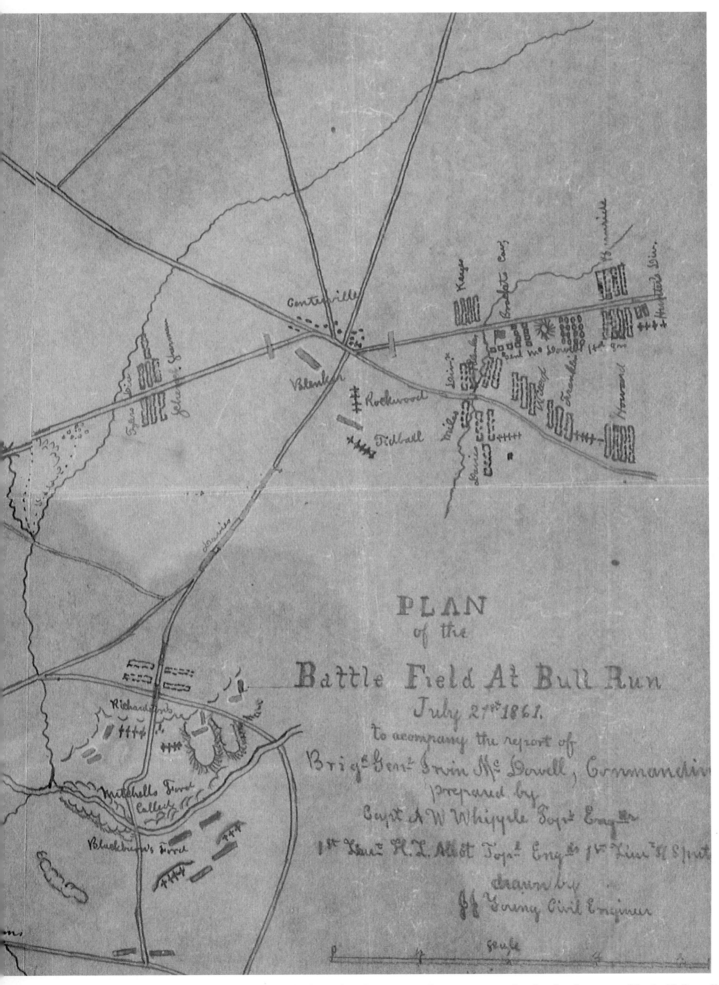

PLAN
of the

Battle Field At Bull Run
July 21st 1861.

to accompany the report of
Brigr Genl Irvin McDowell, Commanding

prepared by
Capt A W Whipple Topl Engrs
1st Lieut H L Abbot Topl Engrs 1st Lieut H S Putnam

drawn by
J J Young Civil Engineer

scale

FIRST BULL RUN. Original, unpublished pen drawing, prepared to accompany the after-battle report of Irvin McDowell, July 21, 1861. The footnote reads "Valuable information in regard to the position of troops. . . ." Scale 1.5 inches=1 mile

THE BATTLE OF SHILOH

April 6–7, 1862

With the loss of Fort Henry and Fort Donelson in February 1862, the Confederates in Tennessee were forced on the defensive. By the end of April, they had lost Nashville. The Union army of Don Carlos Buell, consisting of about 50,000 men, was concentrating its strength there while U. S. Grant was completing his operations in the northwestern corner of the state.

Albert Sidney Johnston, the Confederate commander in Tennessee, had retreated to Murfreesboro with about 20,000 infantry. Pierre G. T. Beauregard, in the western part of the state, was hindered by too few troops. He urged Johnston to concentrate his army, which would soon be reinforced by troops en route from Mobile, Alabama, and parts of Louisiana.

The command structure on both sides was somewhat fluid. Henry Halleck, in Washington, D.C., was attempting to control the movements of Buell's army as well as those of Grant and John Pope, who had 25,000 men in southeastern Missouri. Beauregard, without any troops under his immediate command, was in de facto control of Confederate operations west of the Tennessee River, leaving Johnston in limbo.

Beauregard counseled concentrating troops at Corinth, Mississippi, the site of a vital rail junction near the Tennessee border. By March 29, the Confederates had assembled 40,000 troops at Corinth. Daniel Ruggles, with 5,000 men, had come up the Mississippi River to Memphis, Tennessee, and started his march. Braxton Bragg had brought 10,000 troops from Mobile, and Leonidas Polk had marched from Columbus, Kentucky, with an additional 8,000 men, joining Johnston's 17,000-man force.

On March 11, Grant's army of 35,000 men had come down the Tennessee River and arrived at Crump's Landing, about twenty miles from Corinth. Buell's command had left Nashville on March 16 but had moved only as far as Columbia, Tennessee, on the Duck River. Pope's 25,000 men had, by then, embarked on the campaign for Island No. 10, in the Mississippi River. Halleck could better have used Pope in another capacity, especially considering the smallness of the Confederate garrison at Island No. 10.

After his arrival, Grant had concentrated his army near Shiloh Church, and by the night of April 5, five of his divisions were encamped there. The sixth division, under William Harvey L. Wallace, was covering the area around Crump's Landing, five miles to Grant's rear. The advance division of Buell's army, under William Nelson, was on the opposite bank of the Tennessee River, at Savannah, Tennessee. Grant's division commanders included William T. Sherman, Wallace, John McClernand, Stephen A. Hurlbut, and Benjamin Prentiss.

Grant, lulled into complacency by his misjudgment of Confederate intentions and his underestimation of Confederate capabilities, wired Washington on April 5: "I have scarcely the faintest idea of an attack being made upon us, but will be prepared should such a thing take place." The attitude of his subordinates, notably Sherman, reinforced Grant's thinking.

With the arrival of Johnston's troops at Corinth, Beauregard convinced Johnston that the Confederates must take the offensive. The Confederate army was then organized into four corps: I Corps under Polk, II Corps under Bragg, III Corps under William J. Hardee, and the reserve corps under a former vice

Above: Aerial view of the Tennessee River and the Shiloh battlefield. Dot: Pittsburgh Landing.
Left: The skeletal remains of soldiers many long months after the battle.

SHILOH (or Pittsburg Landing): The initial Confederate attack overruns the Federal camps of Prentiss (1) and Sherman (2). McClernand (3) and Sherman (4) partially stabilize the situation on the right about 9 A.M. and then withdraw as far as the River Road in reasonably good order, under the weight of repeated assaults by Polk and Hardee which endanger their flanks. About 2:30 Johnston is hit (5) while spurring the Southern charge on the Peach Orchard, and Beauregard assumes over-all command. As Breckinridge and Bragg collapse the Union left, the Hornet's Nest becomes an isolated salient (6). After some six hours of savage fighting, Prentiss, finding himself nearly surrounded, surrenders his division at 5:30. By this time, however, Grant has patched together a defensive line (7), studded with artillery, guarding Pittsburg Landing. With the aid of cannon fire from the gunboats *Lexington* and *Tyler* (8), the final Rebel assault is thrown back. As dusk falls Federal reinforcements under Don Carlos Buell begin to arrive (9) from across the Tennessee River, and Lew Wallace's "lost division" (10) finally comes up on the right. Thus strengthened by three fresh Union divisions, Grant attacks the next day and by 4:00 P.M. on April 7 recaptures all of the lost ground.

OWL CREEK

CREEK

SHILOH

First Day: April 6, 1862

RIVER ROAD

Pittsburg
Landing

TENNESSEE RIVER

David Greenspan

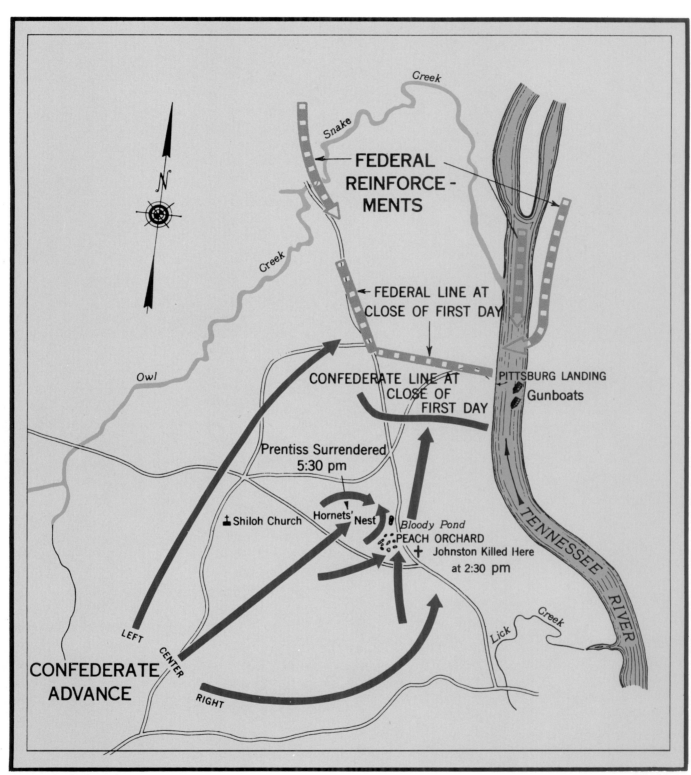

First day positions, April 6, 1862. Confederate-red, Union-blue.

president of the United States, John C. Breckinridge. The total was 40,000 men.

The Confederate advance began on April 3 and quickly found itself hampered with too many troops moving along difficult and inadequate roads. The effort to concentrate the army and remain undetected proved most difficult, and the attack, originally scheduled for April 4, was postponed to April 6. Grant remained oblivious to the impending Southern onslaught. Johnston's plan of attack involved breaking through Grant's left, forcing him back from Pittsburg Landing, Tennessee, and putting the Owl and Snake creeks at his back.

At 6:00 A.M. on April 6, the Confederates charged, catching many Union soldiers totally unprepared in their camps. At the close of battle on that day, Beauregard, who had replaced the slain Johnston in command, felt that victory was within the South's grasp. Grant's army had been battered and all but driven from the field, but as the night passed, the bulk of Buell's army,

three fresh divisions, crossed the Tennessee River. And at daybreak on April 7, the Union forces initiated their own attack.

Buell's men occupied the left of the Federal line. They commenced the action by attacking Hardee's and Breckinridge's troops and immediately were involved in heavy fighting. Sherman and the remainder of Grant's troops on the right flank attacked shortly after Buell's men, initially striking at the forces led by Bragg. With 25,000 fresh troops, the Federals proved too strong, and the Confederates were forced back by degrees, forming, by midafternoon, a defensive line near Shiloh Church.

At this point, Beauregard had decided that his army must retreat, and under the protection of a rear-guard force commanded by Breckinridge, the Confederates withdrew to Corinth. The casualties in this, the first major battle in the west, had been staggering. Total Union losses topped 13,000 out of about 60,000 combatants. Confederate losses were over 25 percent: 10,700 men out of 40,000.

Maj. Gen. Ulysses S. Grant

Maj. Gen. William T. Sherman

Maj. Gen. John. A. McClernand

Gen. A. S. Johnston

Gen. Leonidas Polk

Gen. William J. Hardee

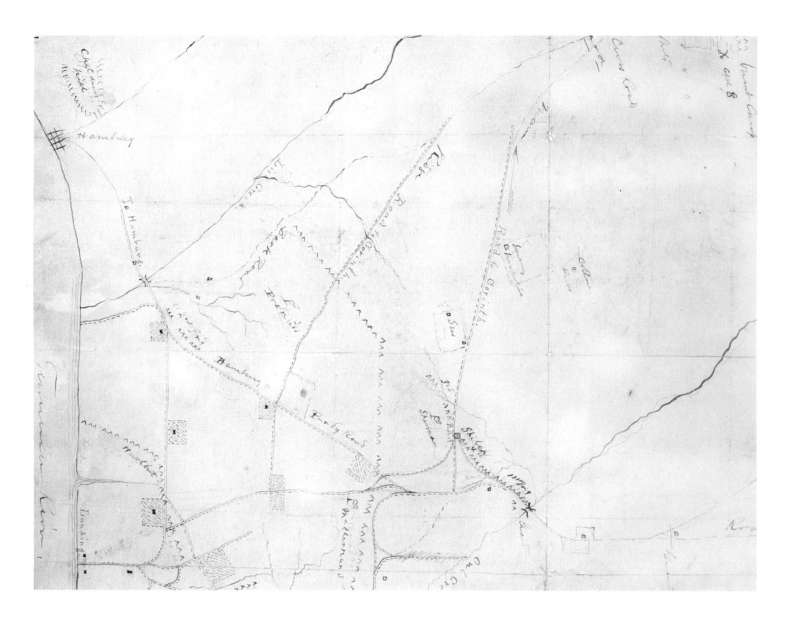

Above: SHILOH. Original, unpublished map of Shiloh battlefield, drawn after the battle by William T. Sherman.

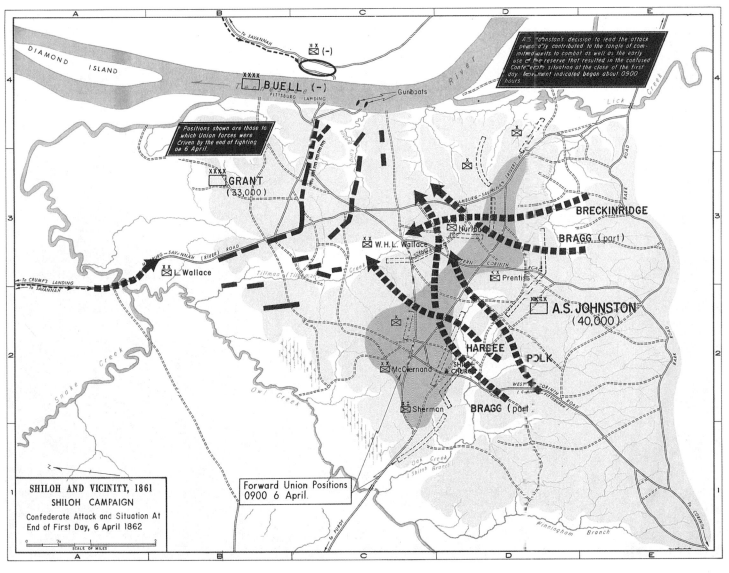

To Savannah

DIAMOND ISLAND

River

Lick Creek

BUELL (-)
PITTSBURG LANDING

Gunboats

As Johnston's decision to lead the attack personally contributed to the tangle of committed units to combat as well as the early use of the reserve that resulted in the confused Confederate situation at the close of the first day. Movement indicated began about 0900 hours.

Positions shown are those to which Union forces were driven by the end of fighting on 6 April.

GRANT
(33,000)

Hamburg-Savannah (River) Road

To Crump's Landing
To Savannah

L. Wallace

Tilghman (Thompson) Creek

Hurlbut

BRECKINRIDGE

BRAGG (part)

W.H.L. Wallace

Eastern Corinth

Hamburg-Savannah (River) Road

Prentiss

A.S. JOHNSTON
(40,000)

Snake Creek

Owl Creek

McClernand

HARDEE

POLK

SHILOH CHURCH

West Corinth

Sherman

BRAGG (part)

Bark Road

Oak Creek (Shiloh Branch)

To Purdy

Locust

Corinth Road (Pittsburgh)

To Corinth

Pinningham Branch

N

SHILOH AND VICINITY, 1861
SHILOH CAMPAIGN
Confederate Attack and Situation At
End of First Day, 6 April 1862

0   ½   1   2
SCALE OF MILES

Forward Union Positions
0900 6 April.

TABLE OF SYMBOLS

BASIC SYMBOLS

Regiment	III	Infantry
Brigade	X	Cavalry
Division	XX	Cavalry Covering Force
Corps	XXX	Artillery
Army	XXXX	Artillery In Position (Does not indicate type or quantity)
		Trains

EXAMPLES OF COMBINATIONS OF BASIC SYMBOLS

Barksdale's Infantry Brigade of McLaws' Division	Barksdale (McLaws)
Stuart's Cavalry Division Minus Detachments	Stuart (-)
First Corps	
Rosecrans' Army of the Cumberland	CUMBERLAND ROSECRANS

OTHER SYMBOLS

Actual position	Prior location	
Troops on the march		Troops displacing and direction
Troops in position		Troops in position under attack
Troops in bivouac or reserve		Route of march
		Strong prepared positions
		Battle Sites

THE SHENANDOAH VALLEY CAMPAIGN

March 23–June 9, 1862

After the campaign of First Manassas, all was quiet in Virginia's Shenandoah Valley for several months. In November 1861, Stonewall Jackson was assigned to command what the Confederates termed "the Valley District." Reinforced by the Stonewall brigade and, later, by 6,000 troops under William W. Loring, Jackson's mission was to prevent Union incursions into the Valley and to protect the left flank of Joseph E. Johnston's army, then concentrated around Centreville, Virginia. The Shenandoah Valley was important as a source of foodstuffs for the Confederate armies and provided invading Southern troops a protected route into western Maryland and Pennsylvania.

Jackson was initially opposed by Nathaniel P. Banks's V Corps, stationed in western Maryland, and by scattered detachments under William S. Rosecrans, primarily in western Virginia (now West Virginia). Rosecrans's outposts tempted Jackson into a winter campaign aimed at capturing those troops at Romney and Bath, West Virginia. Both garrisons escaped. In turn, Jackson occupied Romney with troops of Loring's command. Commander and troops alike were displeased by the decision, and the resulting "Jackson-Loring" controversy nearly ended Jackson's military career.

An appeal by Loring directly to the Confederate Secretary of War resulted in an order that Jackson withdraw the garrison. Jackson, having assumed that his authority in the Valley District was absolute, tendered his resignation. Only the intervention of Johnston calmed the situation.

With the opening of the spring campaign of 1862, Banks's corps operated under the control of George B. McClellan. Directed by McClellan to protect the Baltimore & Ohio Railroad and Chesapeake & Ohio Canal, Banks moved south of the Potomac River and occupied Winchester, Virginia, on March 12.

As McClellan's army embarked for the Peninsula, Banks began a concerted movement up the Shenandoah Valley, led by James Shields's division. Jackson, with fewer than 4,000 troops, aimed to harass Banks's 23,000 troops and prevent a detachment from that command from assisting McClellan. Shields's troops had advanced as far south as Strasburg, Virginia, driving Jackson before them. With Jackson supposedly out of the way, Shields's 9,000 troops were left at Winchester as Banks withdrew toward Washington, D.C.

Following a faulty intelligence report by cavalryman Turner Ashby, Jackson, with his command now numbering about 4,200 men, determined to attack Shields. The resulting Battle of Kernstown, on March 23, ended in a tactical defeat for the Confederates. On a strategic level, however, the battle was an unmitigated success. The authorities in Washington, misinterpreting Jackson's aggressiveness as a sign of strength, ordered Banks back to the Shenandoah Valley.

An additional benefit to the Confederates was Lincoln's decision to retain Irvin McDowell's I Corps near Washington, allowing only a portion of it to join McClellan on the Peninsula. Other units were diverted from the Army of the Potomac, much to McClellan's exasperation. Confederate strength had grown to 6,000 troops, and Jackson then gained control over Richard S. Ewell's division of 8,000 men and the 3,000 men of Edward Johnson, who were deployed near Staunton, Virginia. Banks, with 15,000 troops, occupied New Market and Harrisonburg, Virginia. Another 15,000 men were scattered in western Virginia and near Winchester to the north. A small detachment under Robert Milroy was stationed at McDowell, Virginia.

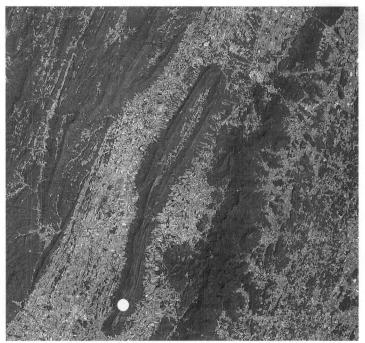

Above: The Shenandoah Valley shown in a satellite photo taken at a height of 438 miles. 1 inch=10 miles. Dot: Cross Keys
Left: Old Jack by Don Troiani, depicting Stonewall Jackson during the Shenandoah Valley Campaign of 1862.

THE SHENANDOAH VALLEY: This lovely region of rich farms nestled amid blue-shadowed mountains played a crucial role in the war. During most of the conflict it served the Confederacy as a vital source of food and forage. Beyond that, geography made it an important military highway, a great "covered way" for the Southern forces. Shielded on the east by the Blue Ridge Mountains, whose gaps were easily screened from prying eyes by cavalry, a Rebel army could march straight down toward the Northern heartland. Conversely, any Union army marching up the Valley would be headed away from Richmond. In 1862 it was the scene of Jackson's great campaign; in 1864 the North's high command decided on a policy of total war and ordered General Philip Sheridan to put the South's granary to the torch. When he finished, the Valley was a scene of blackened desolation.

THE VALLEY

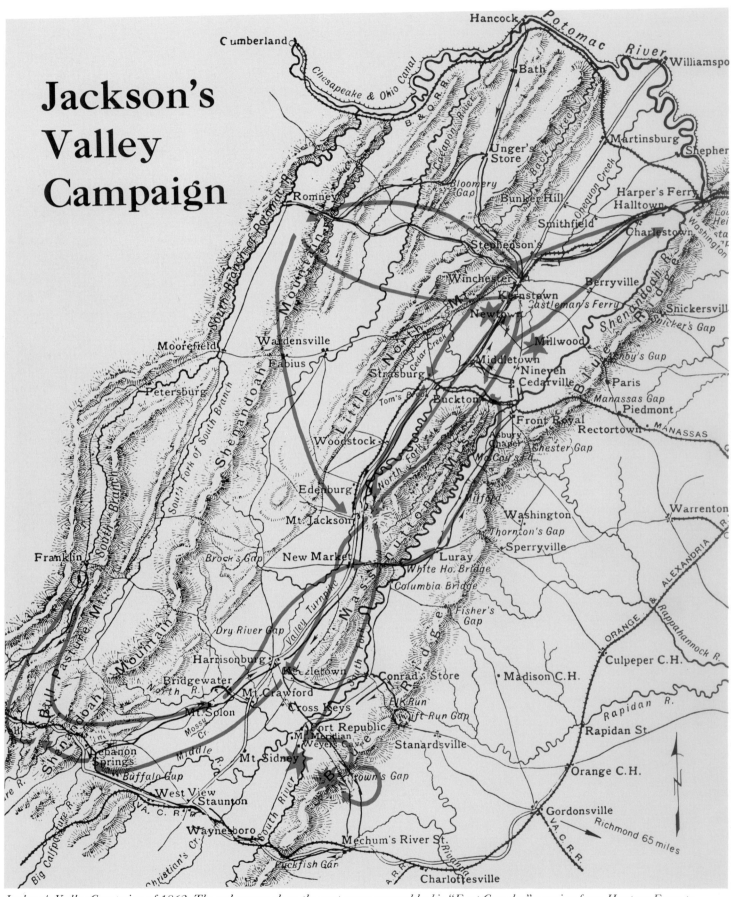

Jackson's Valley Campaign of 1862. The red arrow show the vast areas covered by his "Foot Cavalry" ranging from Harpers Ferry to Brown's Gap, Virginia.

Jackson decided to destroy Milroy and moved his 6,000 infantry to effect a junction with Johnson at Westview, Virginia, between Staunton and McDowell. On May 8, Jackson engaged Milroy and Robert Schenck in a battle at McDowell. Though Jackson maintained the defensive with superior numbers, Schenck undertook an attack and inflicted heavy losses on the Confederates. Jackson, however, repulsed the attack, pursued briefly, and then turned north toward Harrisonburg and Banks's main army. Ewell's division, left behind at Gordonsville, Virginia, became involved in a small controversy when Robert E. Lee attempted to issue orders for it to raid Banks's communications.

Johnston, still in actual command of Confederate forces in Virginia, countermanded Lee's directive and ordered that Ewell cooperate with Jackson or withdraw to Fredericksburg, with the actions of Banks to dictate which course he should pursue.

By May 20, Banks had concentrated his 8,000 men at Strasburg and Front Royal, Virginia (Shields's 10,000-man division having been ordered to McDowell's corps), while John C. Frémont had concentrated his 15,000 troops at Franklin, Virginia. Jackson, with 10,000 men, was at New Market, and Ewell's 6,000 were at Luray, Virginia. When Shields departed, Johnston agreed to leave Ewell with Jackson. The "Valley Campaign" was about to begin in earnest.

Poorly served by his intelligence operatives and cavalry, Banks had no solid idea of Jackson's dispositions. On May 21, Jackson left New Market and, moving into the Luray Valley, joined with Ewell for a march on Front Royal. In the first of a series of lightning marches and surprise movements, the Confederates fell upon the small Union command at Front Royal on May 23 and routed it. Jackson then moved toward Winchester with the bulk of his army, hoping to place himself astride Banks's lines of communication. A stout rear-guard action by George H. Gordon enabled Banks's army to gain Winchester before Jackson cut the Shenandoah Valley turnpike. A further stand by Banks's army on May 25, south of Winchester, resulted in a Union defeat, as Jackson, with equal forces, now proved himself more than a match for Banks and his subordinates.

The Union command, sensing this, canceled McDowell's orders to move to the Peninsula and ordered him to send 20,000 troops to Banks. Frémont, initially ordered to move to Harrisonburg at Jackson's rear, moved to Moorefield, then toward Strasburg. Shields, in the lead division of McDowell's reinforcements, captured Front Royal on May 30. Now Jackson was in real trouble.

Countermarching from Winchester immediately, and with the able assistance of Ashby's cavalry, Jackson slipped the trap at Strasburg. McDowell and Frémont joined forces at Strasburg and headed south after Jackson on June 2. By June 7, Jackson, pursued by the Union forces, had occupied Cross Keys and Port Republic, Virginia. Frémont moved southward via the Shenandoah Valley turnpike. Shields (McDowell's I Corps) moved through the Luray Valley. Jackson's 15,000 troops fell upon Frémont at Cross Keys on June 8 and defeated his force. On June 9, Jackson countermarched and attacked Shields, who, unlike Frémont, was considerably outnumbered. He defeated Shields (and in effect McDowell's command) in a battle thought, nonetheless, to have been mismanaged on the Confederate side. The Union forces withdrew to lick their wounds, and Jackson concentrated his army at Brown's Gap, where it remained until ordered to Richmond on June 17. The "Valley Campaign" was over. It had deprived McClellan's army of much of the reinforcements it would have found so valuable in the developing Peninsular Campaign.

Left to right: Maj. Gen. John C. Frémont, Maj. Gen. Nathaniel Banks, Gen. Thomas J. Jackson , Maj. Gen. Richard S. Ewell

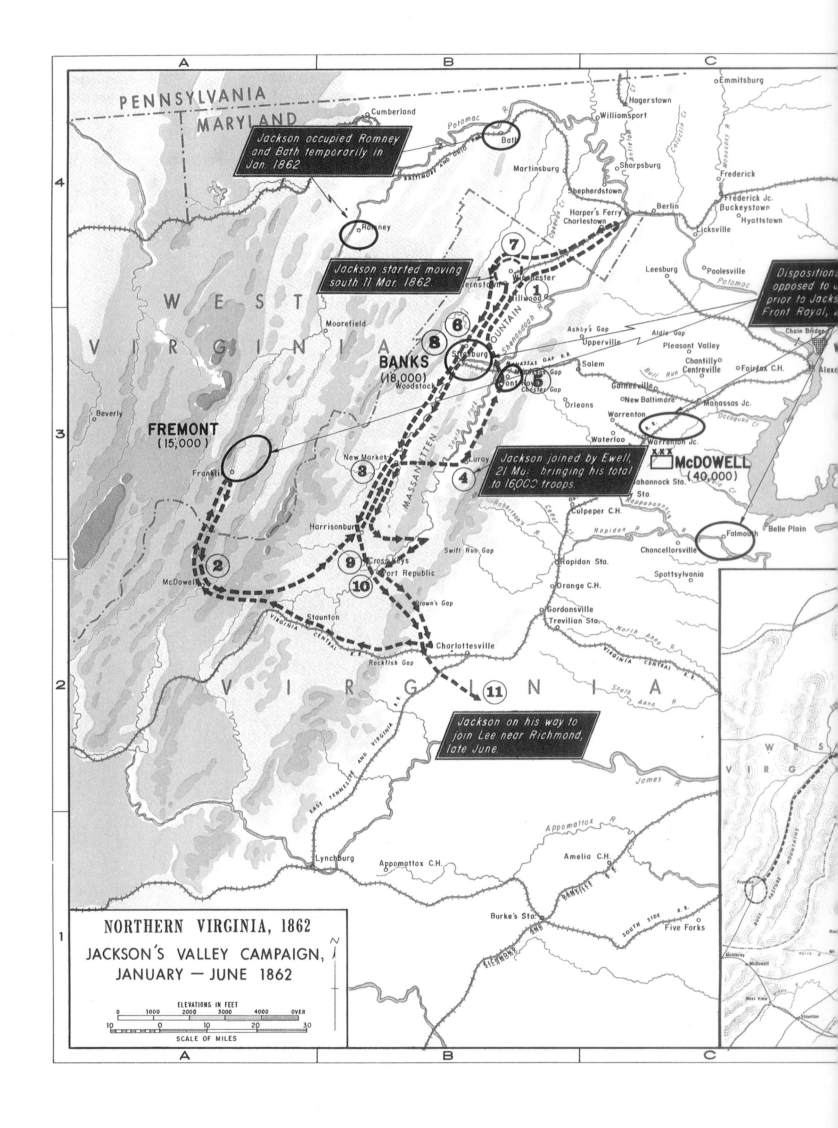

PENNSYLVANIA

MARYLAND

WEST VIRGINIA

VIRGINIA

Jackson occupied Romney and Bath temporarily in Jan. 1862

Jackson started moving south 11 Mar. 1862

Jackson joined by Ewell, 21 Ma. bringing his total to 16000 troops.

Jackson on his way to join Lee near Richmond, late June.

Dispositions opposed to J prior to Jacks Front Royal,

BANKS (18,000)

FREMONT (15,000)

McDOWELL (40,000)

NORTHERN VIRGINIA, 1862

JACKSON'S VALLEY CAMPAIGN,
JANUARY — JUNE 1862

ELEVATIONS IN FEET
0   1000   2000   3000   4000   OVER

10   0   10   20   30
SCALE OF MILES

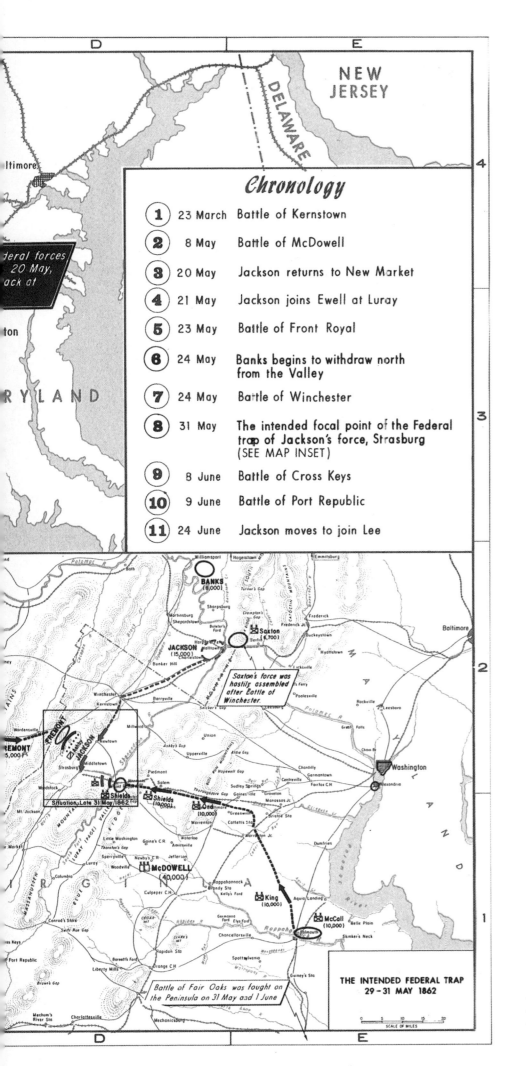

NEW JERSEY

DELAWARE

MARYLAND

(SEE MAP INSET)

Chronology

1	23 March	Battle of Kernstown
2	8 May	Battle of McDowell
3	20 May	Jackson returns to New Market
4	21 May	Jackson joins Ewell at Luray
5	23 May	Battle of Front Royal
6	24 May	Banks begins to withdraw north from the Valley
7	24 May	Battle of Winchester
8	31 May	The intended focal point of the Federal trap of Jackson's force, Strasburg (SEE MAP INSET)
9	8 June	Battle of Cross Keys
10	9 June	Battle of Port Republic
11	24 June	Jackson moves to join Lee

Saxton's force was hastily assembled after Battle of Winchester.

Situation, Late 31 May 1862

Battle of Fair Oaks was fought on the Peninsula on 31 May and 1 June

THE INTENDED FEDERAL TRAP
29 – 31 MAY 1862

SCALE OF MILES

TABLE OF SYMBOLS

BASIC SYMBOLS

Regiment	...		Infantry	
Brigade	...		Cavalry	
Division	...		Cavalry Covering Force	
Corps	...		Artillery	
Army	...		Artillery In Position (Does not indicate type or quantity)	
			Trains	

EXAMPLES OF COMBINATIONS OF BASIC SYMBOLS

Barksdale's Infantry Brigade of McLaws' Division — Barksdale (McLaws)

Stuart's Cavalry Division Minus Detachments — Stuart (–)

First Corps

Rosecrans' Army of the Cumberland — CUMBERLAND ROSECRANS

OTHER SYMBOLS

	Actual location	Prior location	Troops displacing and direction	
Troops on the march				
Troops in position			Route of march	
Troops in bivouac or reserve			Strong prepared positions	
			Battle Sites	

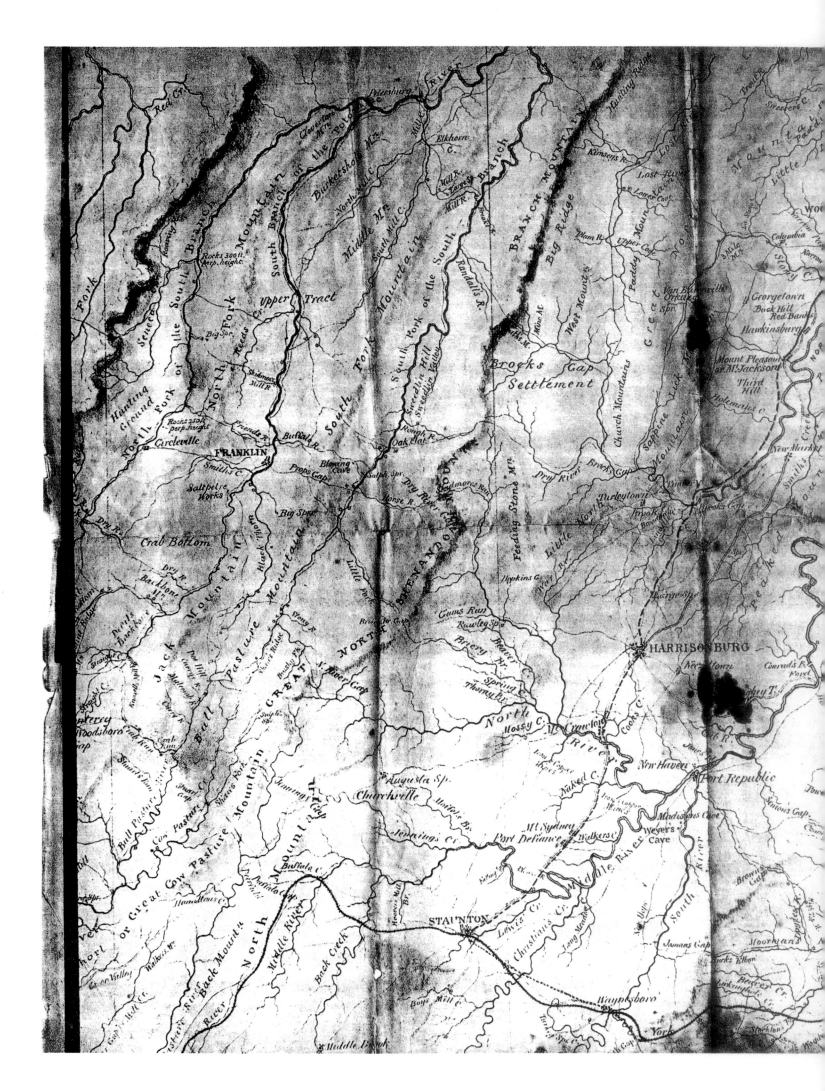

SHENANDOAH VALLEY:
This undated and unpublished map
names every creek, no matter how small,
and gives the double names for towns
and locations that had wartime significance;
for example, "Mt. Pleasant or Mt. Jackson," (center)
or "Culpepper (C. H. far right) or FAIRFAX."

THE PENINSULAR CAMPAIGN

March 17–July 3, 1862

In the spring of 1862, after a winter of inactivity in northern Virginia, as well as on the Peninsula below Richmond, the Union government pressed its commanders for action. George B. McClellan, in command of the Army of the Potomac since the day after the battle of First Manassas, had methodically created a well-trained and superbly equipped fighting force. But McClellan had yet to take the offensive.

McClellan's field army totaled 110,000 men, with an additional 45,000 available for the garrisoning of Washington, D.C. Union general John Wool, with 12,000 men, was occupying Fort Monroe, at the tip of the Peninsula formed by Virginia's James and York rivers.

The Confederates, under Joseph E. Johnston, had withdrawn from Centreville, Virginia (near Manassas Junction), on March 9. Johnston had about 45,000 men, with an additional 22,000 holding the line on the Peninsula and in the city of Norfolk, Virginia. Detachments under Stonewall Jackson and Edward Johnson opposed large Union units commanded by John C. Frémont and Nathaniel P. Banks in western Virginia.

McClellan's plan of operations, begun on March 17, involved transporting his army down the Potomac River. The Union forces embarked at Fort Monroe and advanced on Richmond via the Peninsula. Three Union army corps, totaling 58,000 men—IV Corps, under Erasmus Keyes; II Corps, under Edwin Sumner; and III Corps, under Samuel P. Heintzelman—had arrived at Fort Monroe on April 2, accompanied by McClellan himself.

Confederate forces under John B. Magruder had thrown up entrenchments to the northwest of the Warwick River and in front of Yorktown, Virginia. This force, initially numbering fewer than 15,000 men, fought the Union advance, begun on April 4, to a standstill. McClellan, deceived by Magruder's bold stand, and knowing reinforcements would arrive from Johnston's army, surrendered the initiative and laid siege to Yorktown. After a month of watching the Union forces install heavy siege guns, Johnston withdrew from the Yorktown line on the night of May 3 and began retreating up the Peninsula. On May 5, his rear guard, under Longstreet, and the Union advance forces clashed in a bloody one-day fight at Williamsburg, Virginia. The Confederates continued to withdraw in good order. On May 7, Johnston's troops repulsed a Union amphibious landing at West Point, Virginia, and finally evacuated Norfolk.

As McClellan advanced, he expected Irvin McDowell's I Corps, poised near Fredericksburg, Virginia, to advance against Richmond. However, Jackson's brilliant Shenandoah Valley Campaign, in full swing by May 23, caused the Corps to be diverted toward Front Royal, Virginia.

By May 24, Johnston's 60,000 troops were concentrated around Richmond. Union intelligence agents wrongly estimated this force at 200,000, dwarfing McClellan's 105,000-man army. Caution and continual requests for reinforcements marked McClellan's operations henceforth.

Additionally, the dispositions of his troops were unsound. Three of his five corps were north of the Chickahominy River. Of the remaining two corps, one—IV Corps, under Keyes—held an advance position near Seven Pines, Virginia; the other—Heintzelman's III Corps—was to the rear of this force but not within easy supporting distance. McClellan's positions invited attack, and Johnston, under pressure from his own government, obliged on May 31.

A. P. Hill's division, anticipating support from the commands of Longstreet and Benjamin Huger, attacked Keyes's IV Corps. Keyes was reinforced by Heintzelman, while belated

Above: Area of Mechanicsville Battlefield as seen today.
Dot: National Battlefield Park
Left: Soldier of Co. D, U.S. Sharpshooters, 1862 *by Don Troiani*

43

WOODBURY'S BRIDGE

PORTER'S HQ

LEE'S HQ

Old Cold Harbor

New Cold Harbor

GAINES' MILL

June 27, 1862

GAINES' MILL

N

MECHANICSVILLE

June 26, 1862

ELLERSON'S MILL

Beaver Dam Creek

MECHANICSVILLE: Porter's Yankees contain A. P. Hill's frontal attacks (1 and 2) at Beaver Dam Creek, an assault doomed by Jackson's failure to move against the Union flank (3). Porter pulls back that night. GAINES' MILL: A. P. Hill (1) is repulsed at 2 P.M., and so is Longstreet's diversion (2) two hours later. The divisions of D. H. Hill (3) and Ewell (4) hit the Union right about 4:30, but are driven off with heavy losses. At 5:30 an all-out charge led by John B. Hood's Texans breaches the Union center (5). A Federal cavalry countercharge (6) fails, and Porter retreats across the Chickahominy bridges (7).

Mechanicsville

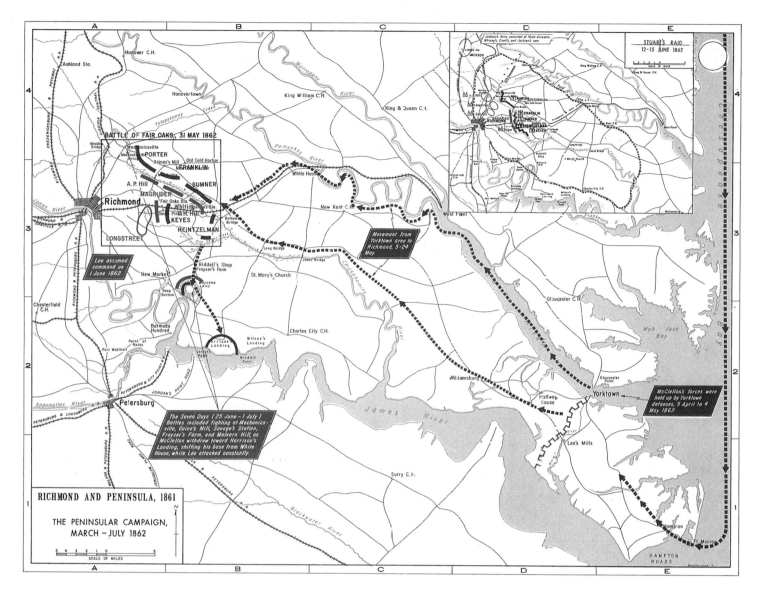

support from Longstreet enabled Hill to dislodge the Union forces. During this fight, Johnston was badly wounded and relinquished command to Gustavus W. Smith.

The Confederates attempted to press the attack on June 1, but with little success. That same day, another change in the command of the Army of Northern Virginia took place. The appointment of Robert E. Lee began a near legendary associa-tion, one that would last for almost three years.

Lee immediately improved the fortifications of Richmond and hounded the Davis administration for reinforcements in order that he might take the offensive. Coastal garrisons and other reserve commands yielded enough troops to bring Lee's strength to 80,000. McClellan also had been reinforced, his forces once again numbering approximately 100,000.

Left to Right:, Gen. Robert E. Lee, Major Gen. A. P. Hill, Major Gen. George B. McClellan, Major Gen. Fitz-John Porter

MALVERN HILL

July 1, 1862

MALVERN HOUSE

PORTER'S HQ

TO HARRISON'S LANDING

WEST HOUSE

CREW HOUSE

WILLIS CHURCH

NELSON HOUSE

QUAKER ROAD

FRAYSER'S FARM

FRAYSER'S FARM

June 30, 1862

LONG BRIDGE ROAD

RIVER

FRAYSER'S FARM: Longstreet and A. P. Hill (1) attack Mc-Call's Union division, capturing McCall himself before being stopped. They then hit Kearny (2) but again are halted. Jackson fails to advance on Long Bridge Road (3), permitting the Federal army to escape to Malvern Hill on the Quaker Road (4). MALVERN HILL: Union artillery knocks out the Rebel guns; then shatters Confederate infantry attacks on the Federal center (1) and left (2), aided by fire from the gunboats (3). McClellan retreats (4) to Harrison's Landing.

Federal troops stream onto the Peninsula from their transports in Hampton Roads.

Eager to take the offensive, Lee sent his cavalry, under Jeb Stuart, to gather information on Union dispositions. Stuart rode unmolested around the entire Union army. His daring maneuver caused McClellan to lose faith in his ability to keep open his lines of communication with Washington, D.C. As a result of this, on June 18, McClellan prepared to move his base of operations to the James River.

Again McClellan divided his army by placing Fitz-John Porter's V Corps on the north bank of the Chickahominy and the remaining four corps on the south bank. With Jackson moving to join him, Lee determined to attack Porter's men with the bulk of his army, leaving only Magruder's and Huger's divisions between McClellan's main body and Richmond.

McClellan's hesitation made this less of a gamble than it might have appeared. McClellan, knowing of Jackson's approach, vacillated between a local attack near the village of Fair Oaks, Virginia, and reinforcing Porter's corps on the north bank of the James. June 25 passed with no activity on the Union side. McClellan put off a decision until the next day.

On the morning of June 26, Lee opened the Seven Days' battles.

Left to Right: Maj. Gen. James Longstreet, Maj. Gen. D. H. Hill

Left: Aerial view of Seven Days battle area showing a portion of the James River at Deep Bottom Landing.
Dot: Deep Bottom Landing

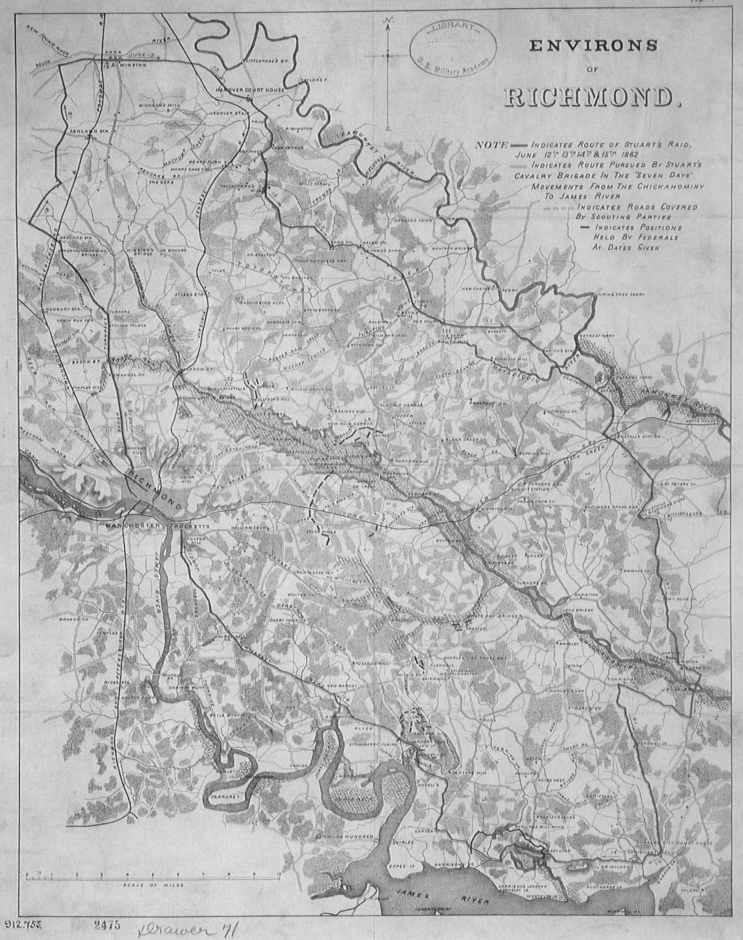

ENVIRONS
OF
RICHMOND.

NOTE ——— INDICATES ROUTE OF STUART'S RAID,
JUNE 12TH 13TH 14TH & 15TH 1862
——— INDICATES ROUTE PURSUED BY STUART'S
CAVALRY BRIGADE IN THE "SEVEN DAYS"
MOVEMENTS FROM THE CHICKAHOMINY
TO JAMES RIVER
——— INDICATES ROADS COVERED
BY SCOUTING PARTIES
— INDICATES POSITIONS
HELD BY FEDERALS
AT DATES GIVEN

SCALE OF MILES

JAMES RIVER

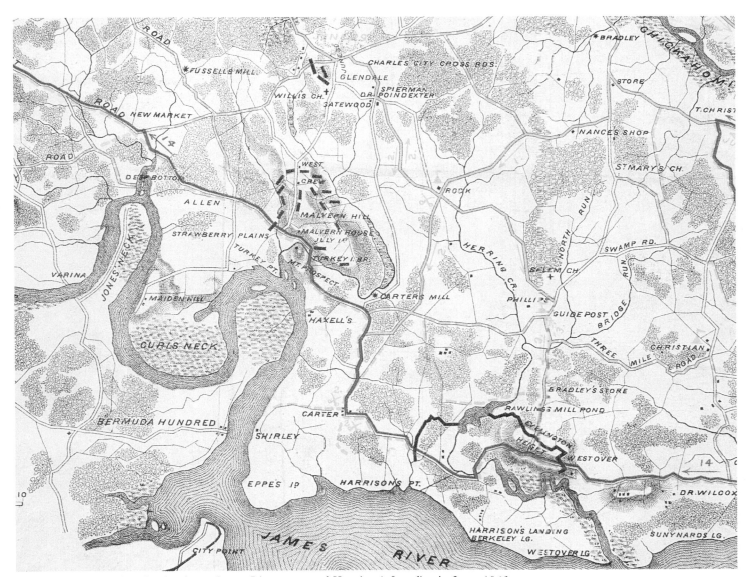

Detail of map opposite, showing lower James River area and Harrison's Landing in June, 1962.

Left: PENINSULAR CAMPAIGN. The area covers the James River and Harrison's Landing in the south, to the juncture of the South Anna and Pamunky rivers in the north. Scale appears to be 1 inch = 1 mile.
Above: Detail of Harrison's Landing area.

THE SECOND BATTLE OF BULL RUN
(Second Manassas)

August 29–30, 1862

With George B. McClellan's army forced back to its base at Harrison's Landing, Virginia, Robert E. Lee looked northward, preparing to counter the second Union threat to Richmond, the newly created Union Army of Virginia, under John Pope. That army, officially created the day of the assault at Mechanicsville, Virginia, numbered some 47,000 men, divided into three corps and commanded by John C. Frémont (soon replaced by Franz Sigel), Nathaniel P. Banks, and Irvin McDowell. The cavalry was an organic outgrowth of the corps rather than a single body of formally assigned horsemen, hence, not under direct control of army headquarters.

Pope's army was created primarily to safeguard Washington, D.C., as well as to ensure that the Confederates could not use the northern part of the Shenandoah Valley and to draw Confederate troops from Richmond by threatening Gordonsville, Virginia. By July 19, Pope's troops were concentrated east of the Blue Ridge Mountains, with Sigel and Banks near Sperryville, Virginia. McDowell's command was charged with guarding Falmouth and Warrenton Junction. Stonewall Jackson, with 12,000 men, had been detached to guard Gordonsville, a key Confederate railhead.

Above: Aerial photo of the same terrain as the first battle of Bull Run. Dot: Stone House.
Left: Bull Run early in the war.

Though Lee's army was greatly weakened by the losses in the Seven Days' battles and by the detachment of Jackson, McClellan refused to take the offensive, choosing to remain at Harrison's Landing. As long as McClellan occupied that position, Lee was not free to move against Pope, whose treatment of the civilian population led Lee to christen him "that miscreant." However, it was thought that if Jackson could be heavily reinforced, he might be able to defeat Pope, then rejoin Lee for a fresh offensive against the Army of the Potomac. This, then, became Lee's broad plan of campaign.

A. P. Hill's veteran division, 12,000 strong, moved to join Jackson on July 27. A countermove by the Union army brought Ambrose Burnside's IX Corps (14,000 men) by boat from Fortress Monroe to Fredericksburg, Virginia, arriving there on August 5. In concert with this movement, McClellan went on a brief offensive near Malvern Hill. When Lee moved out to do battle, the Union forces retreated.

In Washington, Henry Halleck now decided to withdraw the Army of the Potomac from the Peninsula and put it into the field in northern Virginia, uniting with Pope. Jackson, knowing that Lee would begin to move north with the balance of the Army of Northern Virginia, began a forward movement from Gordonsville. Pope, unwilling to give ground until McClellan's troops were north of the Rappahannock River, had moved Banks's corps to Cedar Mountain, a position that threatened Gordonsville. There, on the afternoon of August 9, Jackson's troops and Banks's corps fought a fierce and inconclusive action. Jackson held the battlefield until August 12, then fell back to Gordonsville. With McClellan's withdrawal progressing and the threat to Richmond lessening daily, Lee, on August 14, sent James Longstreet to reinforce Jackson, leaving only two of Lee's brigades on the Peninsula.

The morning of August 17 found Pope and Lee, each with 55,000 troops, facing each other across the Rapidan River near Cedar Mountain. A plan by Lee to turn Pope's left was aborted by Pope's eventual withdrawal and by Confederate logistical problems. By August 22, Pope had withdrawn beyond the Rappahannock, protecting his main line of supply from Manassas Junction. He received the first reinforcements from McClellan's 90,000-man army on that date. Lee, pursuing Pope, began to realize that time was running out if he wanted to strike a blow against the Union's Army of Virginia.

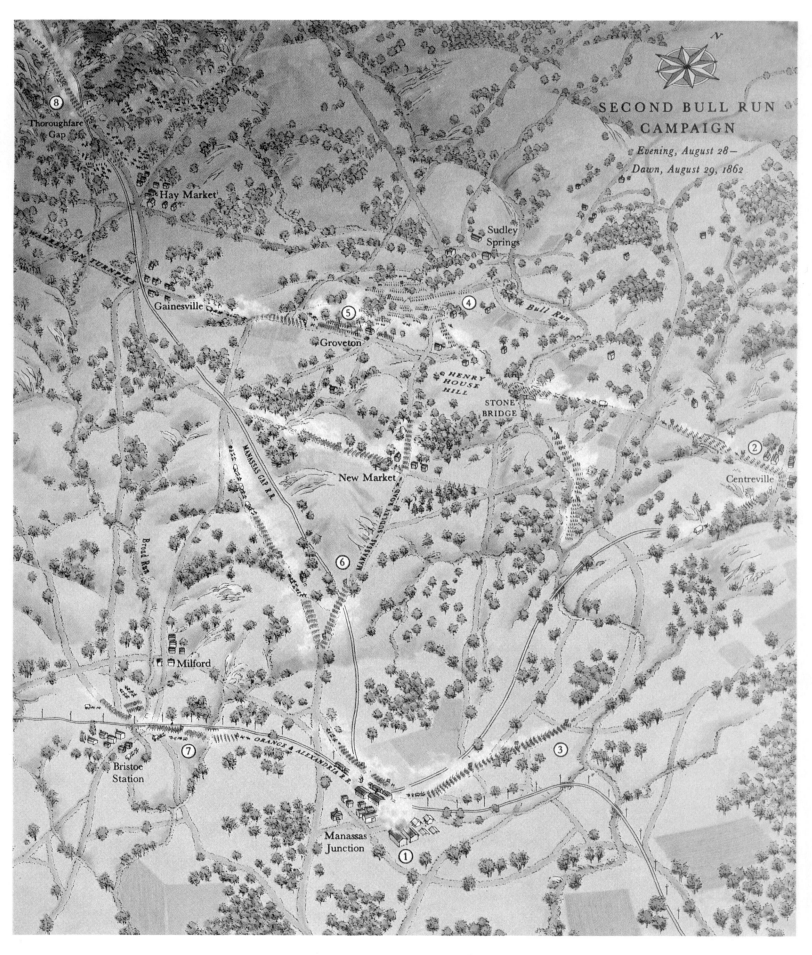

CAMPAIGN OF SECOND BULL RUN: After pillaging Pope's stores at Manassas Junction (1) on August 26, Jackson moves toward Centreville (2), pursued by Heintzelman and Reno (3). Jackson slips away and digs in (4) near Grove-ton on August 28. That evening he attacks King (5), revealing his position. Sigel (6) countermarches, followed by Porter (7). As the various Federal columns converge on Groveton, Longstreet (8) advances to join Jackson.

SECOND BULL RUN

Second Day: August 30, 1862

SUDLEY CHURCH

JACKSON'S HQ

GROVETON — SUDLEY ROAD

①

⑥

UNFINISHED RAILROAD

MATTHEWS HILL

MATTHEWS HOUSE

MANASSAS — SUDLEY ROAD

③

WARRENTON TURNPIKE

POPE'S HQ

STONE HOUSE

veton

②

YOUNG'S BRANCH

ROBINSON HOUSE

TO CENTREVILLE

HENRY HOUSE HILL

STONE BRIDGE

HENRY HOUSE

NN SE

④

BALD HILL

⑤

BULL RUN

wid Greenspan

Second Bull Run (or Manassas): Pope begins the second day's action with an assault (1) on Jackson. Then Longstreet's artillery (2) stuns the Union left, followed by a flank attack (3 and 4) which captures Bald Hill. As the Federals form a new defensive line (5) on the Henry House Hill, Jackson strikes their right wing (6). This patchwork line holds long enough for the rest of the Federal army to escape via the Stone Bridge to Centreville.

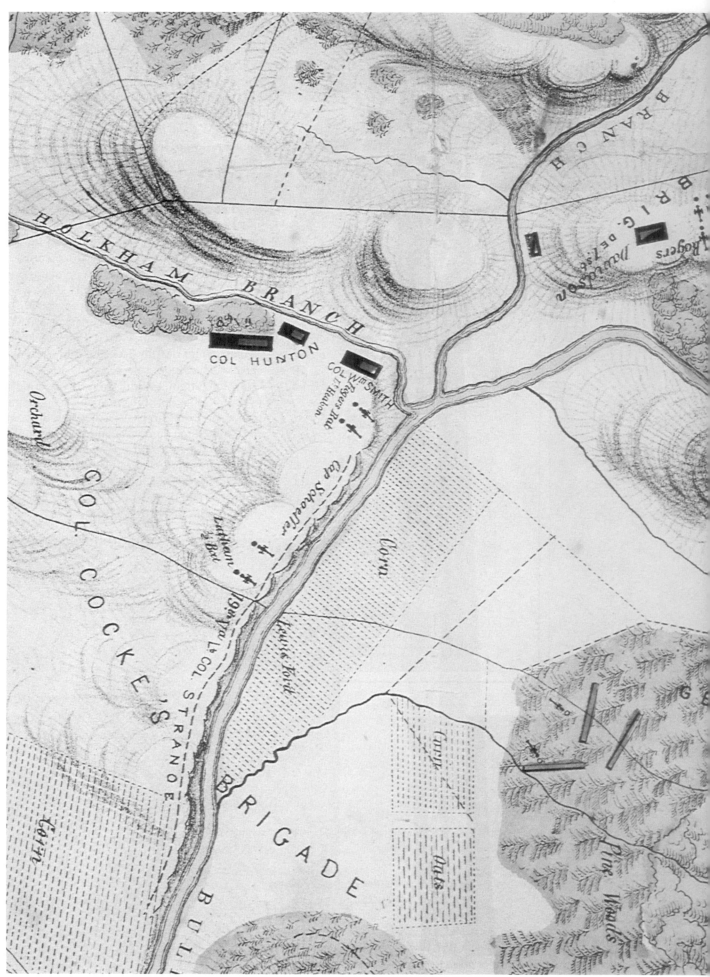

SECOND BULL RUN. Prepared and drawn by Joseph Horner in 1862, ". . . from surveys by an officer of Gnl. Beauregard's Staff." Henry House Hill, which is the first promontory directly below the stone bridge, is, for whatever reason, not noted.

COL EVANS

AYON Tackett

4th S.C. Col Sloan

Nursery Branch

STONE BRIDGE

TURNPIKE

S.C.

SCHENCK'S Bde

warwork

SHERMA

THE BATTLE OF ANTIETAM
(Sharpsburg)

September 17, 1862

The aftermath of the Confederate victory at Second Manassas found John Pope's command broken up and integrated into the Army of the Potomac, with Pope himself reassigned to the Northwest Department.

George B. McClellan worked vigorously to reorganize his new command, now numbering nine corps. These were commanded by: Joseph Hooker (I Corps), Edwin Sumner (II Corps), Samuel P. Heintzelman (III Corps), Erasmus Keyes (IV Corps), Fitz-John Porter (V Corps), William B. Franklin (VI Corps), Jesse L. Reno (IX Corps), Franz Sigel (XI Corps), and Joseph Mansfield (XII Corps). Only Darius Couch's division of IV Corps was with the army at Washington, D.C., while a portion of the division guarded the former Union base at Harrison's Landing, Virginia.

As part of his army, McClellan had also Alfred Pleasonton's cavalry division, bringing McClellan's effective strength to 84,000 men. Another 12,000 troops, under Colonel Dixon S. Miles, were responsible for the defense of Harpers Ferry.

Robert E. Lee concentrated his 55,000 troops around Chantilly, Virginia, and began crossing the Potomac River below Frederick, Maryland, on September 4, 1862. His nine divisions were formed into two corps, I Corps under James Longstreet (with the divisions of Lafayette McLaws, R. H. Anderson, David R. Jones, James G. Walker, and John B. Hood) and II Corps under Stonewall Jackson (with the divisions of Alexander Lawton, A. P. Hill, John R. Jones, and D. H. Hill). The cavalry division under Jeb Stuart screened the entire movement.

By September 7, the Army of Northern Virginia was concentrated around Frederick. Lee, now in enemy territory and outnumbered nearly two to one, once again divided his army and embarked on a bold and dangerous course.

Jackson, less the division of D. H. Hill, was sent to capture Harpers Ferry. Longstreet moved with his command to Boonsboro, Maryland, to await the return of Jackson. A report that the Pennsylvania militia was assembling at Chambersburg caused Lee to dispatch Longstreet and two divisions to Hagerstown, Maryland. Longstreet's remaining troops guarded the South Mountain passes at Turner's Gap and Crampton's Gap. By the evening of September 13, McClellan had marched the bulk of his army to the vicinity of Frederick, within easy striking distance of the passes. During that day, he had come into possession of the now famous "Special Order No. 191," detailing Confederate plans and dispositions.

That night, Franklin (VI Corps) was ordered to Crampton's Gap and Burnside (commanding I Corps and IX Corps) to Turner's Gap. The morning of September 14 found Jackson still besieging Harpers Ferry (which fell the next day) and D. H. Hill defending Turner's Gap.

From Maryland Heights, overlooking Harpers Ferry, McLaws's division moved to defend Crampton's Gap against the Union thrust. Both Confederate commands fought skillfully and forced the much larger Union forces into a slow advance. Longstreet's arrival at South Mountain late in the day allowed the Confederates to hold the pass until late that night.

With the surrender of Harpers Ferry, a good portion of Lee's army (consisting of Jackson with the divisions of Walker, Lawton, John R. Jones, and A. P. Hill) was still south of the Potomac. The loss of the South Mountain passes had forced Lee to begin concentrating his army at Sharpsburg, Maryland, behind Antietam Creek.

Above: Aerial view of the battlefield, with a portion of the town of Sharpsburg and the Potomac River. Dot: Sharpsburg.
Left: Dunker Chuch after the battle.

ANTIETAM

September 17, 1862

LEE'S HQ

TO POTOMAC RIVER

TO HARPERS FERRY

Sharpsburg

⑧

⑥

⑦

BURNSIDE'S BRIDGE

ANTIETAM CREEK

David Greenspan

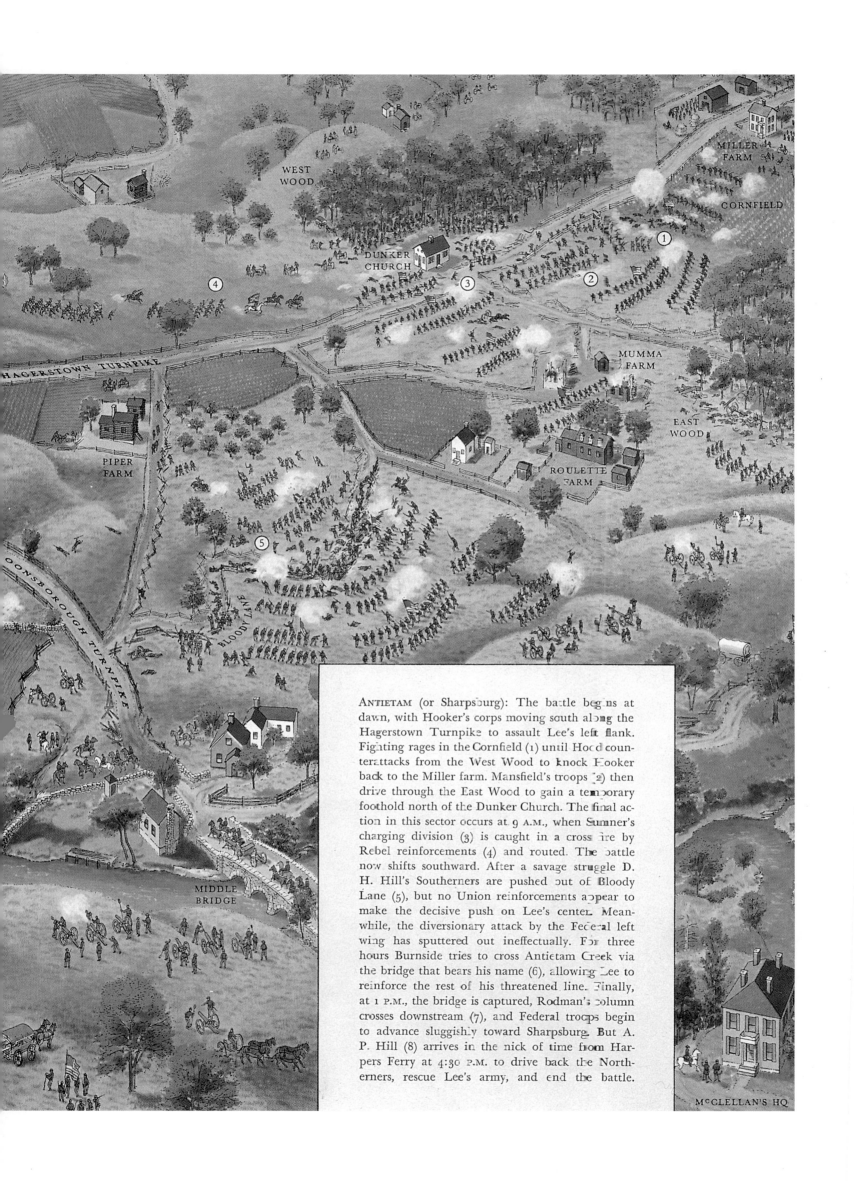

WEST WOOD

MILLER FARM

CORNFIELD

DUNKER CHURCH

HAGERSTOWN TURNPIKE

MUMMA FARM

EAST WOOD

PIPER FARM

ROULETTE FARM

BLOODY LANE

BOONSBOROUGH TURNPIKE

MIDDLE BRIDGE

ANTIETAM (or Sharpsburg): The battle begins at dawn, with Hooker's corps moving south along the Hagerstown Turnpike to assault Lee's left flank. Fighting rages in the Cornfield (1) until Hood counterattacks from the West Wood to knock Hooker back to the Miller farm. Mansfield's troops (2) then drive through the East Wood to gain a temporary foothold north of the Dunker Church. The final action in this sector occurs at 9 A.M., when Sumner's charging division (3) is caught in a cross fire by Rebel reinforcements (4) and routed. The battle now shifts southward. After a savage struggle D. H. Hill's Southerners are pushed out of Bloody Lane (5), but no Union reinforcements appear to make the decisive push on Lee's center. Meanwhile, the diversionary attack by the Federal left wing has sputtered out ineffectually. For three hours Burnside tries to cross Antietam Creek via the bridge that bears his name (6), allowing Lee to reinforce the rest of his threatened line. Finally, at 1 P.M., the bridge is captured, Rodman's column crosses downstream (7), and Federal troops begin to advance sluggishly toward Sharpsburg. But A. P. Hill (8) arrives in the nick of time from Harpers Ferry at 4:30 P.M. to drive back the Northerners, rescue Lee's army, and end the battle.

McCLELLAN'S HQ

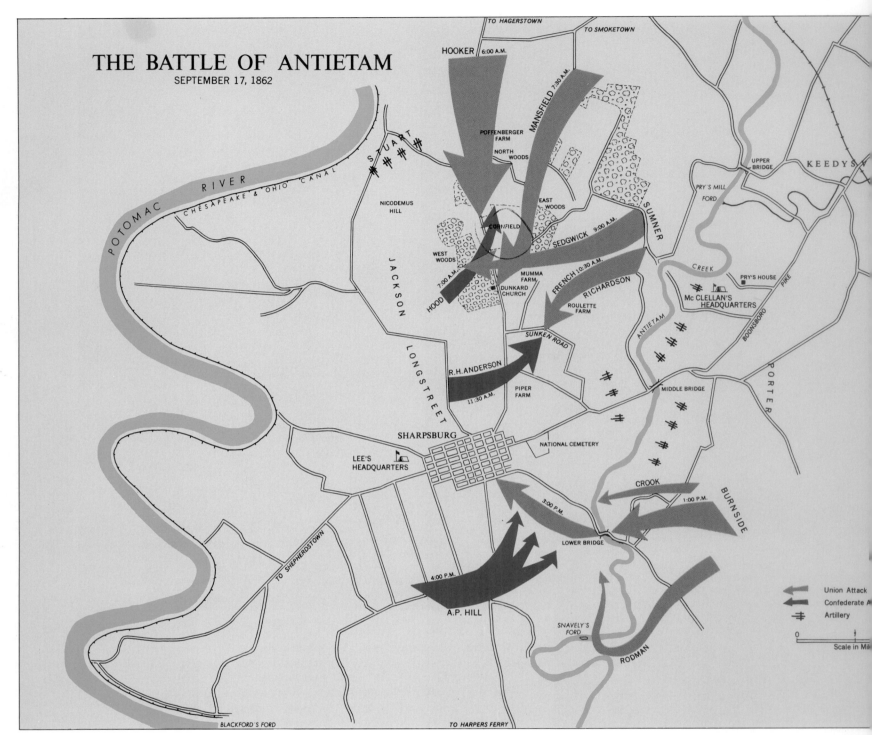

THE BATTLE OF ANTIETAM
SEPTEMBER 17, 1862

TO HAGERSTOWN
TO SMOKETOWN

HOOKER 6:00 A.M.

MANSFIELD 7:30 A.M.

POFFENBERGER FARM

NORTH WOODS

KEEDYS

UPPER BRIDGE

PRY'S MILL FORD

NICODEMUS HILL

EAST WOODS

CORNFIELD

SUMNER

SEDGWICK 9:00 A.M.

PRY'S HOUSE

POTOMAC RIVER

CHESAPEAKE & OHIO CANAL

STUART

WEST WOODS

7:00 A.M.

HOOD

JACKSON

LONGSTREET

MUMMA FARM

DUNKARD CHURCH

FRENCH 10:30 A.M.

RICHARDSON

ROULETTE FARM

SUNKEN ROAD

R.H. ANDERSON

PIPER FARM

11:30 A.M.

McCLELLAN'S HEADQUARTERS

CREEK

ANTIETAM

PORTER

BOONSBORO PIKE

SHARPSBURG

NATIONAL CEMETERY

MIDDLE BRIDGE

LEE'S HEADQUARTERS

CROOK

BURNSIDE

3:00 P.M.

1:00 P.M.

TO SHEPHERDSTOWN

4:00 P.M.

LOWER BRIDGE

A.P. HILL

SNAVELY'S FORD

RODMAN

Union Attack
Confederate A
Artillery

0
Scale in Mil

BLACKFORD'S FORD

TO HARPERS FERRY

Lee considered a withdrawal south of the Potomac, and so he instructed McLaws's division to move across the river to defend Crampton's Gap. With the fall of Harpers Ferry and with Jackson's corps soon to rejoin the army, Lee decided to give battle. His position at Sharpsburg was not a strong one: Antietam Creek was shallow and easily forded at several locations; the high ground on the east bank favored the Union artillery; and the Confederates could cross the Potomac only at Boteler's Ford, in the rear of the extreme right of the Confederate line—a difficult crossing at best.

The bulk of the Union army arrived along Antietam Creek in the early afternoon of September 15. McClellan had four corps—those of Hooker (I), Jacob D. Cox (IX—Reno had been killed at South Mountain), Sumner (II), and Mansfield (XII), along with Pleasonton's cavalry—opposite the Confederate left, held by Hood, D. H. Hill, and Stuart's cavalry. Nearby were two other divisions and Franklin's I Corps. Lee also had on the field the division of David R. Jones.

By the morning of September 16, all of McClellan's army, some 75,000 men, was on the field or within supporting distance. Lee, with the arrival of Jackson and the divisions of Lawton and John R. Jones, mustered about 27,000 troops, with an additional 10,000 men en route from Harpers Ferry. A. P. Hill remained at Harpers Ferry to parole the Union garrison.

The stage was now set for the battle of September 17, a series of uncoordinated attacks by McClellan that resulted in the bloodiest single day of the war.

Left to right:
Gen. Robert E. Lee
Maj. Gen. John B. Hood
Maj. Gen. A. P. Hill
Maj. Gen. George B. McClellan
Maj. Gen. Ambrose E. Burnside
Maj. Gen. Joseph Hooker

TABLE OF SYMBOLS

BASIC SYMBOLS

Regiment	……………… (III)	Infantry	⊠
Brigade	……………… x	Cavalry	⊠
Division	……………… xx	Cavalry Covering Force	• • • • • •
Corps	……………… xxx	Artillery	▣
Army	……………… xxxx	Artillery In Position	▭
		(Does not indicate type or quantity)	
		Trains	⌂

EXAMPLES OF COMBINATIONS OF BASIC SYMBOLS

Barksdale's Infantry Brigade of McLaws' Division — Barksdale (McLaws)

Stuart's Cavalry Division Minus Detachments — Stuart (−)

First Corps — xxx ▭▭▭

Rosecrans' Army of the Cumberland — xxxx CUMBERLAND ROSECRANS

OTHER SYMBOLS

Actual location / Prior location

Troops on the march ……………… ➡ / ⇠⇢

Troops in position ……………… ◗ / ◖

Troops in bivouac or reserve ……………… ◯ / ◯

Troops displacing and direction …

Troops in position under attack …

Route of march ……………… ▪▪▪▪▪

Strong prepared positions ……………… ⊓⊔⊓⊔

Battle Sites ……………… ⚔

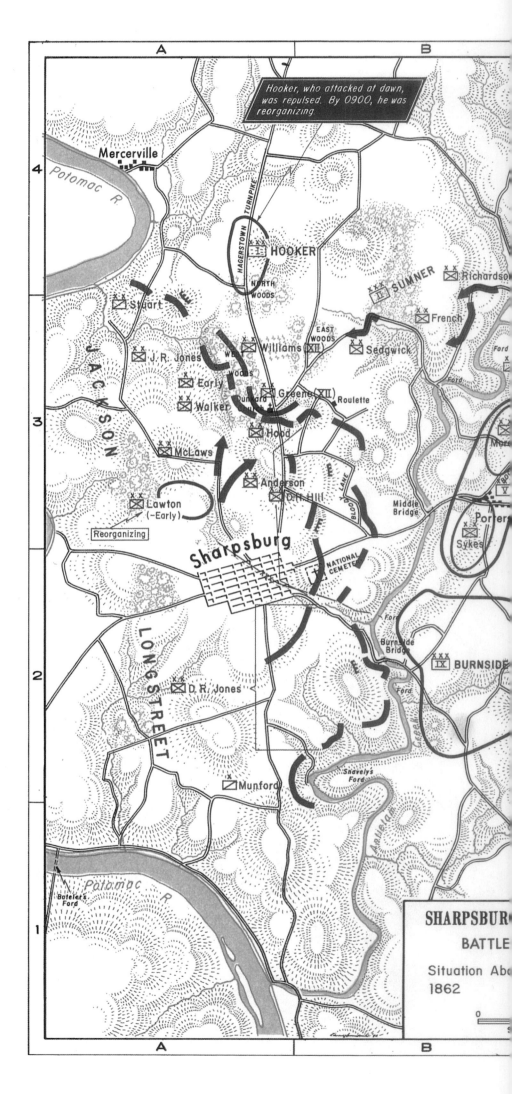

Hooker, who attacked at dawn, was repulsed. By 0900, he was reorganizing.

SHARPSBURG

BATTLE

Situation Abo

1862

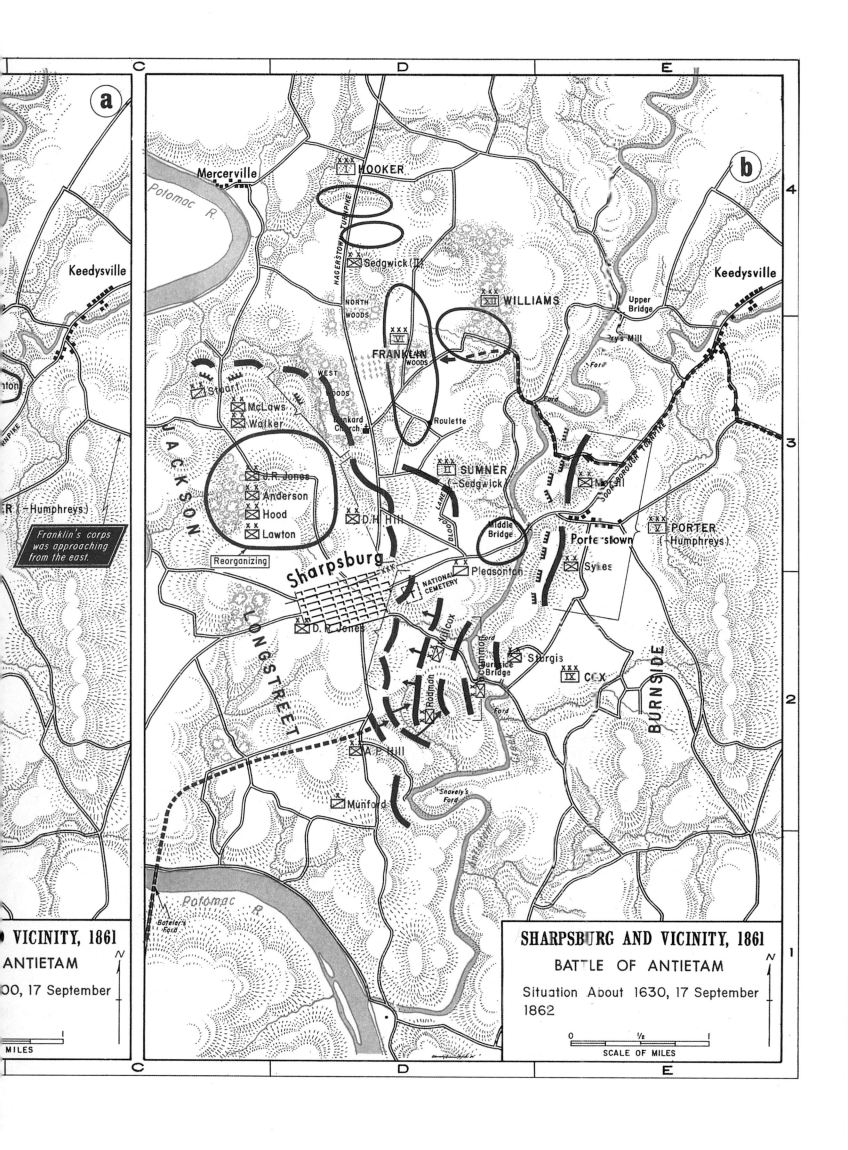

a

Mercerville

Potomac R.

Keedysville

☒☒ Stuart

JACKSON

Franklin's corps
was approaching
from the east.

R. (-Humphreys)

VICINITY, 1861

ANTIETAM

00, 17 September

MILES

☒ HOOKER

HAGERSTOWN TURNPIKE

☒☒ Sedgwick (II)

NORTH
WOODS

WEST
WOODS

☒☒ McLaws

☒☒ Walker

Dunkard
Church

XXX
VI
FRANKLIN
WOODS

Roulette

☒☒ J.R. Jones

☒☒ Anderson

☒☒ Hood

☒☒ Lawton

Reorganizing

☒☒ D.H. Hill

BLOODY LANE

XXX
II SUMNER
(-Sedgwick)

Sharpsburg

☒☒ D.R. Jones

NATIONAL
CEMETERY

XXX
Pleasonton

Willcox

Rodman

Middle
Bridge

Antietam

Burnside
Bridge

Snavely's
Ford

LONGSTREET

☒☒ A.P. Hill

☒☒ Munford

Potomac R.

Boteler's
Ford

XXX
XII WILLIAMS

Upper
Bridge

Keedysville

's Mill

Ford

Ford

BOONSBOROUGH TURNPIKE

☒☒ Meagher

☒☒ Sykes

Porterstown

XXX
V PORTER
(-Humphreys)

☒☒ Sturgis

XXX
IX COX

BURNSIDE

SHARPSBURG AND VICINITY, 1861

BATTLE OF ANTIETAM

Situation About 1630, 17 September
1862

0   ½   1
SCALE OF MILES

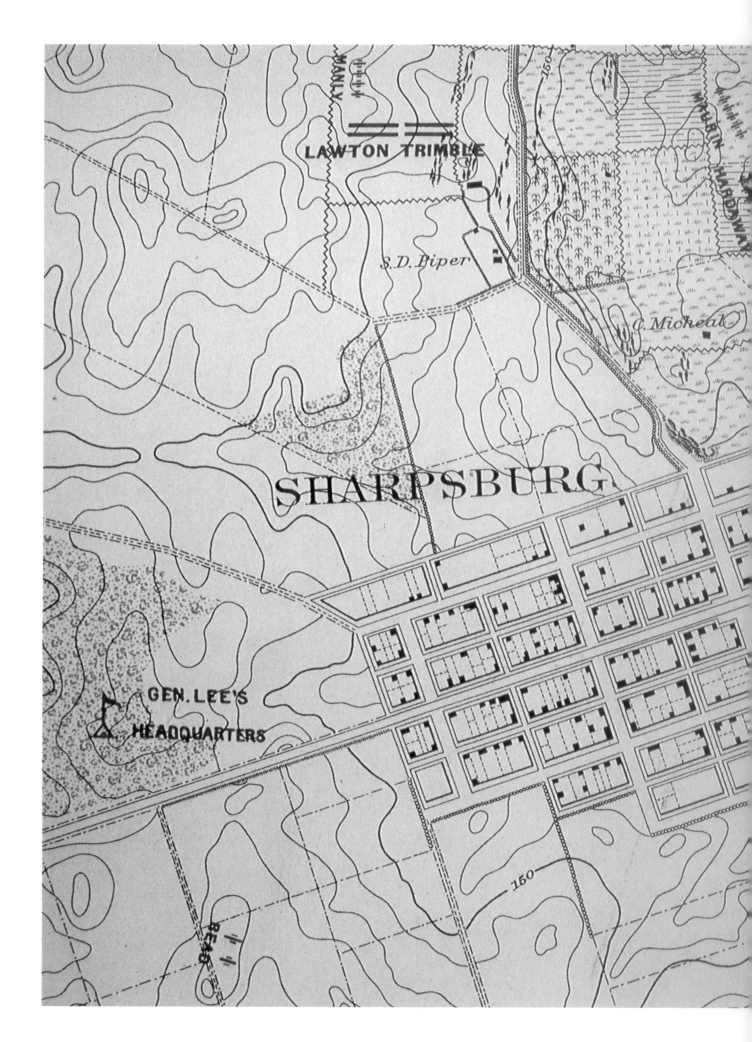

LAWTON TRIMBLE

S.D. Piper

C. Micheal

SHARPSBURG

GEN. LEE'S
HEADQUARTERS

ANTIETAM. The detail is from plate #9 of the 1904 edition of the definitive Atlas of the Battlefield of Antietam, *drawn by Charles H. Ourland. It shows the positions of the combatants from 3:30 to 3:45 PM on September 17, 1862.*

THE BATTLE OF FREDERICKSBURG

December 13, 1862

Lee's invasion of Maryland ended in the bitter, indecisive fighting around Sharpsburg, Maryland. Staggered by their losses, the Confederates nonetheless remained in line of battle on September 18. The following day, Lee began a series of retrograde movements, which, by November 6, brought Stonewall Jackson's corps near Winchester and James Longstreet's to Culpeper Court House, both in Virginia.

George B. McClellan's mismanaged and uncertain pursuit of Lee's army resulted in his being relieved of command on November 7. Ambrose Burnside took command of the Army of the Potomac, which was concentrated in the area about Warrenton, Virginia. The Army of the Potomac was soon reorganized into three grand divisions, which were commanded by Edwin Sumner, Joseph Hooker, and William B. Franklin. A reserve corps (XI) under Franz Sigel, was concentrated near Gainesville, Virginia, along the Manassas Gap Railroad. The Union cavalry screened the Blue Ridge Mountain passes, keeping an eye on Jackson, as well as the various crossings on the Rappahannock River.

Burnside, who had enjoyed some success in independent command on the North Carolina coast in 1862, was not a brilliant soldier—and was not reluctant to admit it. His performance along Antietam Creek had neither enhanced nor diminished his reputation. Unlike his predecessor, McClellan, however, he did not eschew politics, and had proved himself a loyal soldier. He would, above all, be the Lincoln administration's man. Burnside did not seek the command and did not feel qualified for it—most unexhilarating characteristics for an army commander.

The plan of operation that Burnside submitted to Washington, D.C., on November 9 had three main objectives: crossing the Rappahannock at Fredericksburg, Virginia; shifting the base of supply to Aquia Creek and Falmouth; and forcing Lee to concentrate his army south of the Rappahannock. Jackson's corps was still concentrated near Winchester, Virginia. If the Union soldiers moved quickly enough, an opportunity to attack and defeat Longstreet's troops might present itself before Jackson could arrive.

Burnside concentrated the Army of the Potomac near Warrenton and appeared to be threatening Culpeper or Gordonsville, important points on the Orange and Alexandria Railroad. Burnside's transfer of his base of supply would serve to eliminate the threat of Jackson's falling upon his rear as he moved toward Fredericksburg.

Essential to the plan of attack was the arrival of pontoon bridges at Falmouth. which was intended to coincide with the arrival of Burnside's army, now 120,000 strong. President Lincoln approved the plan with the comment, "It will succeed if you move very rapidly, otherwise not."

The Army of the Potomac moved out on November 15, with the lead elements arriving opposite Fredericksburg on November 17. Longstreet's corps was on the march from Culpeper, but at that time, only about 500 Confederates garrisoned the town of Fredericksburg.

Burnside's maneuvering came to naught, however, as the pontoons, slowed by bureaucratic inefficiency, failed to arrive until November 25. Sumner's proposal to ford the river and seize the town directly was rejected by Burnside, who felt that unpredictable winter rains might isolate a portion of the army and expose it to defeat by a superior Confederate force.

On November 21, Longstreet's corps of 35,000 men (divisions of Lafayette McLaws, R. H. Anderson, John B. Hood, George Pickett, and Robert Ransom, Jr.) arrived at Fredericksburg and went into position on Marye's Heights, overlooking the town. Burnside was seized with indecision.

Above: Aerial view of Fredericksburg. Dot: Fredericksburg
Left: Looking west across the Rappahannock River at the town of Fredericksburg, Va. in 1862.

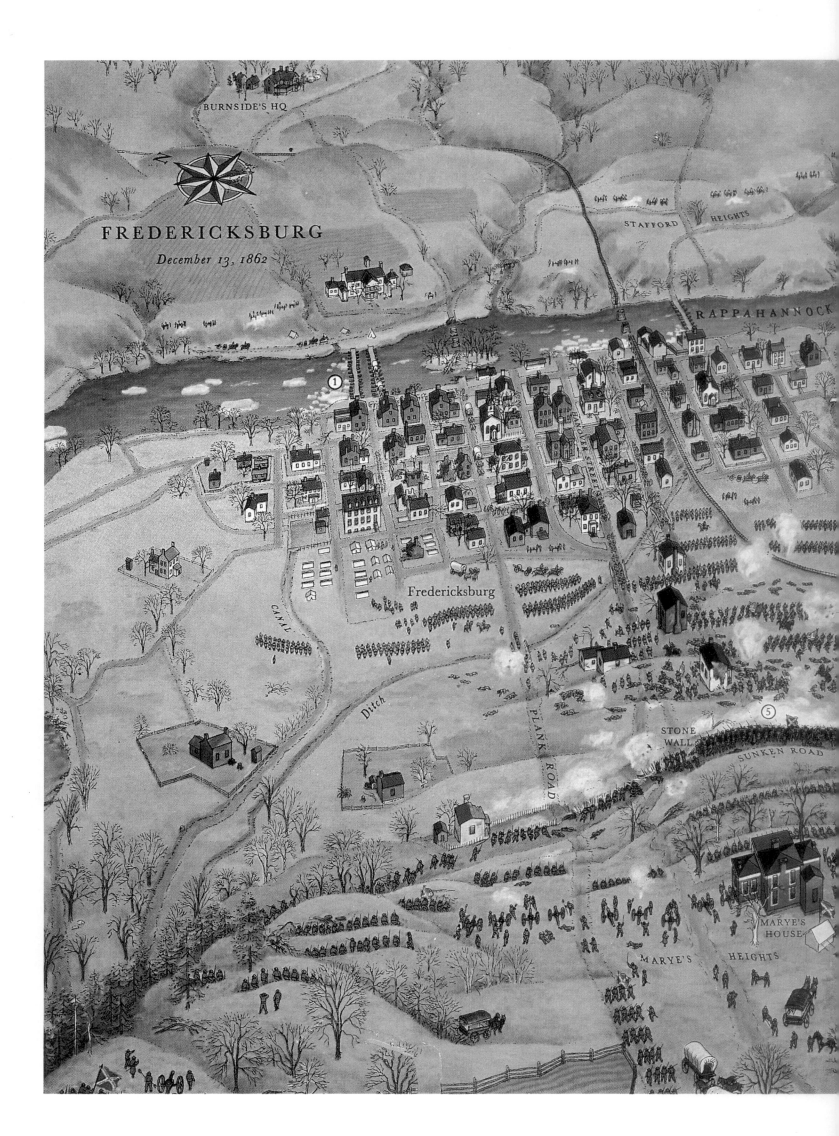

FREDERICKSBURG

December 13, 1862

BURNSIDE'S HQ

STAFFORD HEIGHTS

RAPPAHANNOCK

CANAL

Fredericksburg

Ditch

PLANK ROAD

STONE WALL

SUNKEN ROAD

MARYE'S HOUSE

MARYE'S HEIGHTS

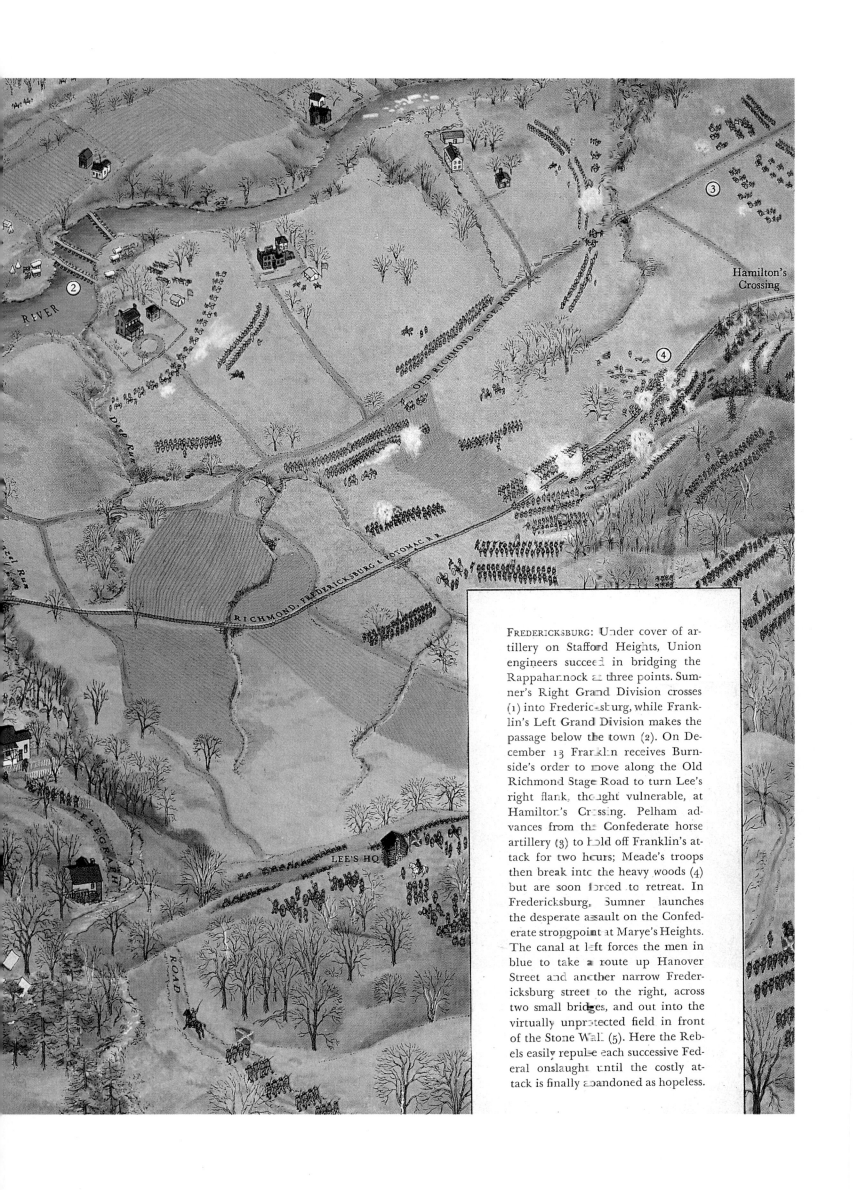

RIVER

Hamilton's
Crossing

② ③ ④

OLD RICHMOND STAGE ROAD

RICHMOND, FREDERICKSBURG & POTOMAC R.R.

TELEGRAPH

LEE'S HQ

ROAD

FREDERICKSBURG: Under cover of artillery on Stafford Heights, Union engineers succeed in bridging the Rappahannock at three points. Sumner's Right Grand Division crosses (1) into Fredericksburg, while Franklin's Left Grand Division makes the passage below the town (2). On December 13 Franklin receives Burnside's order to move along the Old Richmond Stage Road to turn Lee's right flank, thought vulnerable, at Hamilton's Crossing. Pelham advances from the Confederate horse artillery (3) to hold off Franklin's attack for two hours; Meade's troops then break into the heavy woods (4) but are soon forced to retreat. In Fredericksburg, Sumner launches the desperate assault on the Confederate strongpoint at Marye's Heights. The canal at left forces the men in blue to take a route up Hanover Street and another narrow Fredericksburg street to the right, across two small bridges, and out into the virtually unprotected field in front of the Stone Wall (5). Here the Rebels easily repulse each successive Federal onslaught until the costly attack is finally abandoned as hopeless.

Jackson's corps (divisions of D. H. Hill, A. P. Hill, Jubal Early, and William Taliaferro), numbering 35,000, arrived on November 30 and went into position on Longstreet's right, on lower ground and behind the line of the Fredericksburg and Potomac Railroad. Jeb Stuart's cavalry of 5,000 sabers, augmented by Pelham's horse artillery, covered Jackson's flank near Hamilton's Crossing.

On November 25, the pontoons, enough for only one bridge, finally arrived. The shortage of these pontoon bridges forced Burnside to scrap his plan for crossing on November 26. If handled properly, his superior force could have overwhelmed Longstreet's troops, but still Burnside waited. Jackson's arrival on November 30 ended any hopes of an opportunity to defeat the Confederates decisively.

The Union army began its crossings on the night of December 10, with six pontoon bridges at last in place. On the left, Franklin's Grand Division met little opposition. Confederate troops in the town of Fredericksburg, under the command of William Barksdale, contested the Union bridge-building operations with such accurate fire that an amphibious assault by the Union force was required to secure the riverbank. The crossing there was not completed until December 12, under cover of a heavy fog. Well-handled Union artillery on Stafford Heights convinced Lee not to defend the town but to stay where he was and defend the heights.

On December 12, Burnside made a diversionary attack with Sumner on Marye's Heights. The main assault was made by Franklin, supported by Hooker, on the Confederate right, which was held by Jackson. This was followed by Burnside's vague written orders on December 13. Confused, piecemeal Union attacks became the order of the day.

The Army of the Potomac performed with a gallantry worthy of better leadership, suffering 12,000 casualties. The Confederates suffered losses of less than half that. Lee, on watching the massacre of the Union columns, said, "It is well that war is so terrible; men would love it too much."

Maj. Gen. Ambrose E. Burnside

Maj. Gen. Edwin V. Sumner

Maj. Gen. William B. Franklin

Gen. Robert E. Lee

Maj. Gen. Jubal Early

Maj. Gen. D. H. Hill

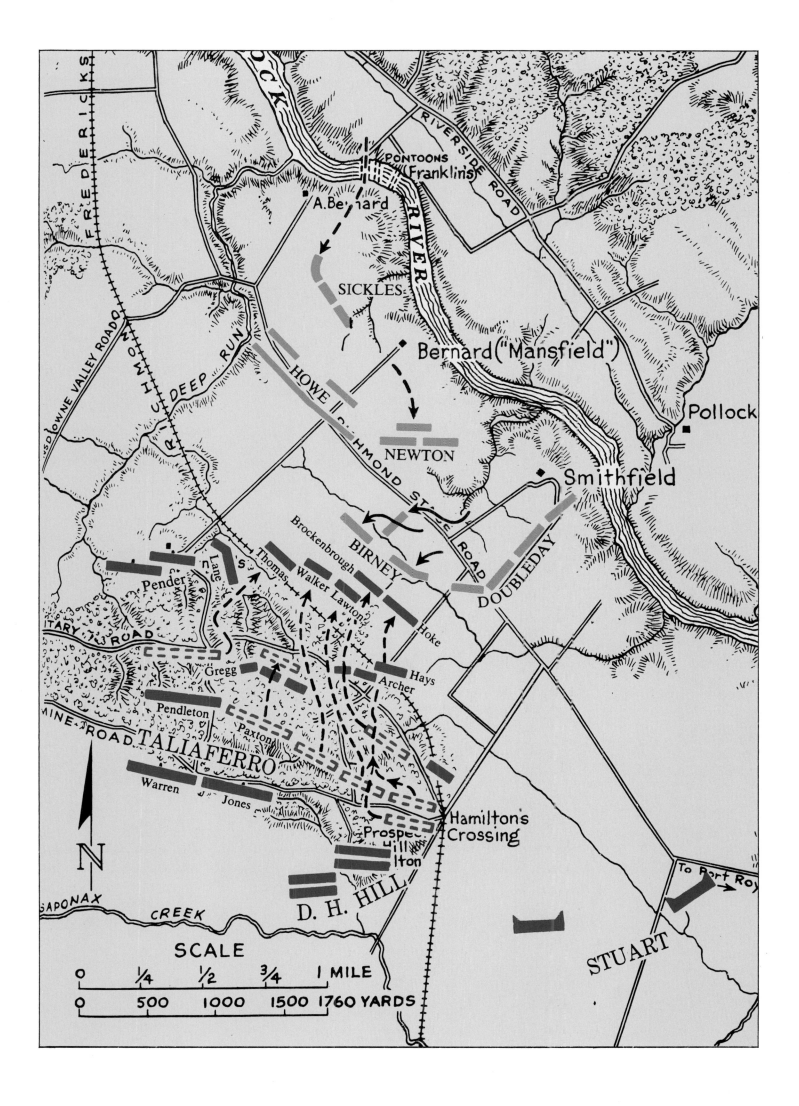

PONTOONS (Franklin's)

A. Bernard

RIVER

RIVERSIDE ROAD

SICKLES

Bernard ("Mansfield")

Pollock

HOWE

RICHMOND

DEEP RUN

FREDERICKS

NY RIVER

LOWNE VALLEY ROAD

NEWTON

Smithfield

STAGE ROAD

Brockenbrough

BIRNEY

DOUBLEDAY

Pender

Lane

's

Thomas

Walker

Lawton

Hoke

TARY ROAD

Gregg

Hays

Archer

Pendleton

Paxton

MINE ROAD

TALIAFERRO

Warren

Jones

Hamilton's
Crossing

Prospect
Hill
lton

N

D. H. HILL

SAPONAX

CREEK

To Port Roy

STUART

SCALE

0   ¼   ½   ¾   1 MILE

0   500   1000   1500 1760 YARDS

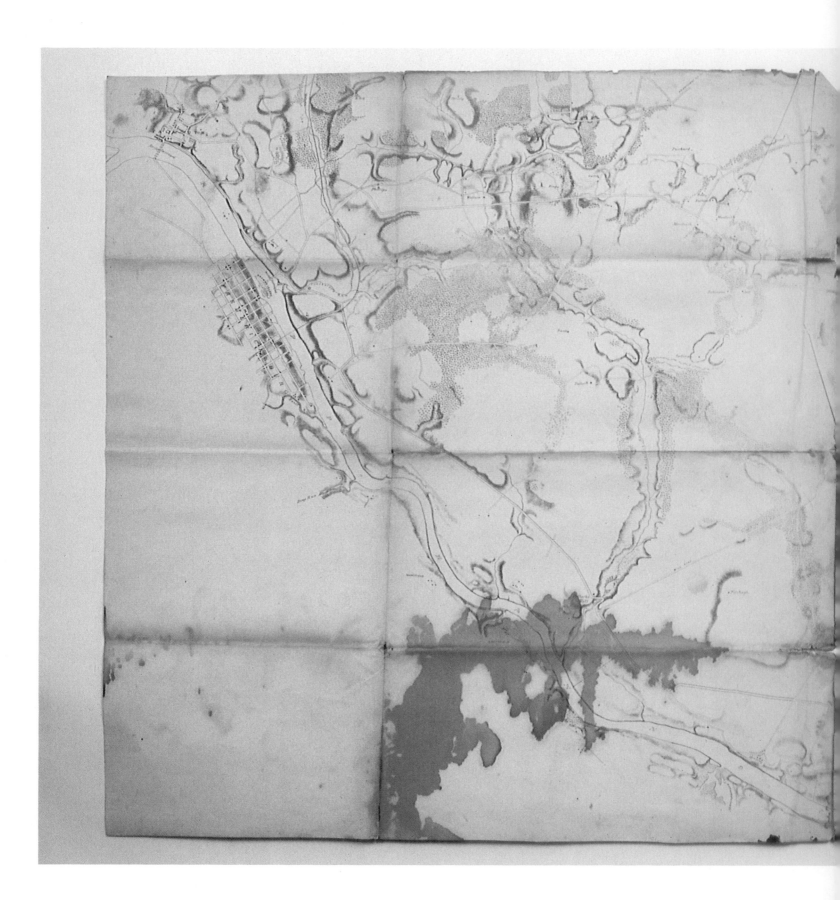

FREDERICKSBURG. The legend reads "Prepared by Bvt. Brig. Genl. N. Michler, Major of Engineers from Surveys under his direction. . . . 1867." Scale: 3 inches=1 mile.

THE BATTLE OF MURFREESBORO
(Stones River)

December 31, 1862–January 2, 1863

Following the abortive Confederate invasion of Kentucky in September and October 1862, Confederate general Braxton Bragg had retreated into Tennessee and regrouped his army near Murfreesboro. His two corps, in five infantry divisions, under William J. Hardee and Leonidas Polk, numbered about 38,000 troops. The position at Murfreesboro, behind the Stones River, was a threat to Nashville, about thirty miles away, and covered the approaches to Chattanooga, a vital point in Confederate east–west rail communications.

Like George B. McClellan in the east, Don Carlos Buell, the Union commander in Kentucky, had failed to initiate a vigorous pursuit of the retreating Confederates. Buell was replaced on October 30, 1862, by William S. Rosecrans, victor of the relatively inconclusive fighting against Earl Van Dorn's troops at Corinth, Mississippi, in early October. Rosecrans was a skilled strategist and appeared eager (as Buell did not) to fight. Henry Halleck, who was giving strategic direction to the war from Washington, D.C., informed Buell that his primary objective was to be the occupation of eastern Tennessee.

Rosecrans moved quickly to reorganize his cavalry corps, which he placed under the command of David S. Stanley, a capable officer. The nine infantry divisions of his Army of the Cumberland were reorganized into three "wings": the left, under Thomas L. Crittenden; the right, under Alexander M. McCook; and the center, under George H. Thomas. Upon its regrouping near Nashville, the Union army totaled 47,000 men.

By the time Rosecrans began his advance, on December 26, Bragg had divided up his army. He had sent much of his cavalry, under John H. Morgan and Nathan Bedford Forrest, against Rosecrans's lines of communication. And he had dispatched Hardee's corps to Triune, Tennessee, about fifteen miles from Murfreesboro. Faced with the Union advance, Bragg quickly recalled Hardee.

Rosecrans's advance was initially conducted in three columns, with Crittenden's wing advancing by the most direct route to Murfreesboro. Thomas's and McCook's wings were to swing around the Confederate left, composed of Hardee's corps, forcing it out of position. The abandonment of the Confederate position at Triune made this unnecessary, and both wings were now directed to Murfreesboro. Bragg's remaining cavalry, under Joseph Wheeler, delayed the advance at every opportunity and kept Bragg well informed of the Union dispositions and movements. The bulk of the Union cavalry was raiding east of the Cumberland Gap, intent upon disrupting Bragg's supply lines. The force remaining with Rosecrans was no match for Wheeler's troopers.

Above: Aerial view of Murfreesboro battlefield. Dot: Cowan House.
Left: Confederate Cavalry Sergeant *by Don Troiani.*

MURFREESBORO

December 31, 1862
January 2, 1863

FIELD OF JANUARY 2ND

BRAGG'S
JAN

STONES RIVER

ROSECRANS'
HQ

NASHVILLE & CHATTANOOGA R.R.

NASHVILLE TURNPIKE

FIELD O

David Greenspan

MURFREESBORO (or Stones River): At dawn on December 31 Bragg launches his sledge-hammer attack near the Widow Smith House, catching some of the Federals at breakfast (1). This assault completely turns the Union right, an entire corps being driven back some three miles before rallying on the Nashville Turnpike. As succeeding waves of Confederates crash through the scrub cedar, men under Phil Sheridan fight valiantly (2) but are forced to retire for lack of ammunition, which has been held up by Rebel cavalry forays at far left. Imperturbable George H. Thomas, whose very glance seemed to freeze would-be skulkers in their tracks, falls back and begins to form a new Union line (3), at right angles to the original one. Astride the railroad tracks, Colonel William B. Hazen's artillery stubbornly holds its original position—the only Union detachment to do so—at the center of the line (4). The first day's battle draws to a close with the Federals formed in a salient around Rosecrans' Headquarters (5). On January 2 Breckinridge is ordered to make a charge across an open field (6), vulnerable to Union artillery at the river's edge. Only when Union reinforcements are hurried across the river (7) is this final Confederate assault halted.

Murfreesboro

GG'S HQ
EC. 31

VAN
USE

WIDOW
SMITH
HOUSE

WILKINSON TURNPIKE

ECEMBER 31ST

GRISCOM
HOUSE

Overall's Creek

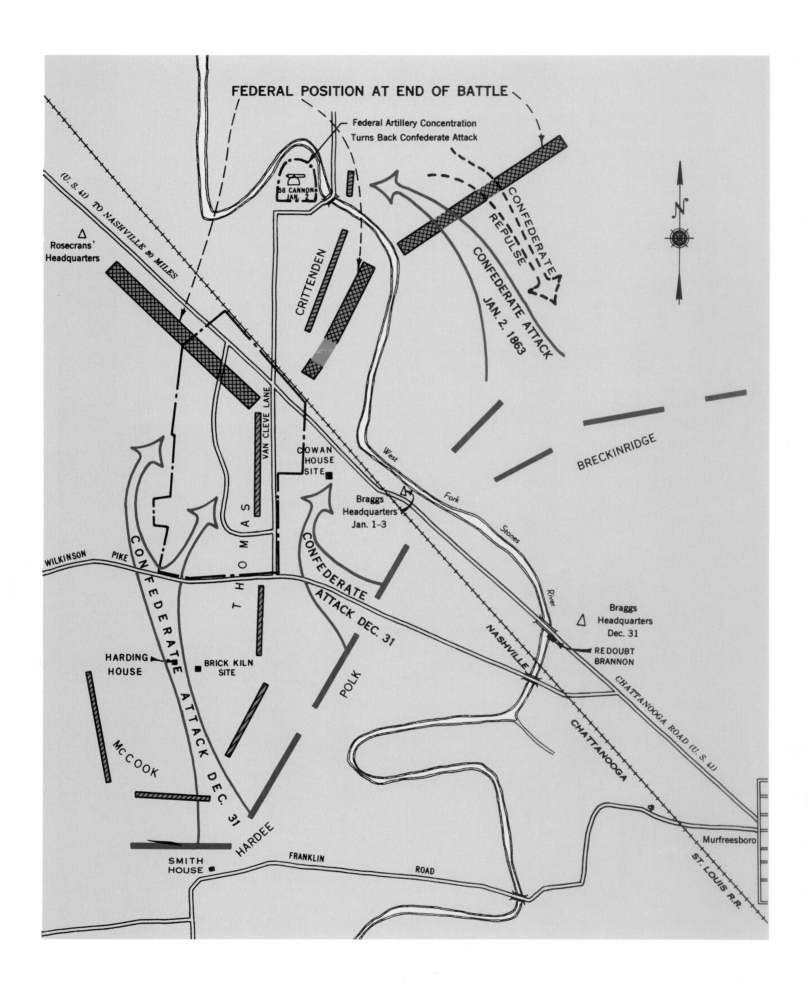

FEDERAL POSITION AT END OF BATTLE

Federal Artillery Concentration
Turns Back Confederate Attack

58 CANNON
JAN. 2

CONFEDERATE
REPULSE

CONFEDERATE ATTACK
JAN. 2, 1863

CRITTENDEN

Rosecrans'
Headquarters

(U. S. 41) TO NASHVILLE 30 MILES

BRECKINRIDGE

VAN CLEVE LANE

COWAN
HOUSE
SITE

West

Fork

Braggs
Headquarters
Jan. 1–3

Stones

THOMAS

WILKINSON   PIKE

CONFEDERATE ATTACK DEC. 31

CONFEDERATE   ATTACK DEC. 31

POLK

River

NASHVILLE

Braggs
Headquarters
Dec. 31

REDOUBT
BRANNON

HARDING
HOUSE

BRICK KILN
SITE

McCOOK

HARDEE

SMITH
HOUSE

FRANKLIN   ROAD

CHATTANOOGA

CHATTANOOGA ROAD (U. S. 41)

Murfreesboro

ST. LOUIS R.R.

Steady rain and fog impeded the Union advance, and Union intelligence about the Confederate forces was scant. Crittenden's wing, reinforced by a division of Thomas's, reached the vicinity of Murfreesboro on the evening of December 29. Thomas's and McCook's wings arrived mid-morning on December 30 and spent the rest of the day going into position.

The Stones River, flowing north to south, split the battlefield in half. The Confederates had posted Polk's corps—consisting of John McCown's, Benjamin Cheatham's, and Jones M. Withers's divisions, and reinforced by Patrick Cleburne's division of Hardee's command—to the west of the river, in a north-south line adjacent to the Widow Smith's house.

Hardee, left with John C. Breckinridge's division, held a position east of the river and north of Murfreesboro. The Union line, about seven-hundred yards distant, ran south and west from the river, and Crittenden's wing, reinforced by Thomas, held the Union left, closest to the river. McCook's wing, consisting of the divisions of Philip H. Sheridan, Jefferson C. Davis (unrelated to the Confederate president), and Richard W. Johnson, held the right. By coincidence, both the opposing generals determined to attack on the morning of December 31, intending to hold back their right wings and initiate the attack with their reinforced left wings. It was for this purpose that Polk had been reinforced by Crittenden and by portions of Thomas's command, with the balance remaining in reserve.

The contending armies were almost evenly matched in manpower, and victory would therefore favor the quickest. Initially, this proved to be the Confederates, but after two days of pitched battle and 12,000 casualties on both sides, Bragg withdrew and began a cold, sodden retreat to Tullahoma, Tennessee, to search for answers.

Maj. Gen. William Rosecrans

Maj. Gen. Thomas L. Crittenden

Maj. Gen. Braxton Bragg

Gen. William J. Hardee

Maj. Gen. Joseph Wheeler

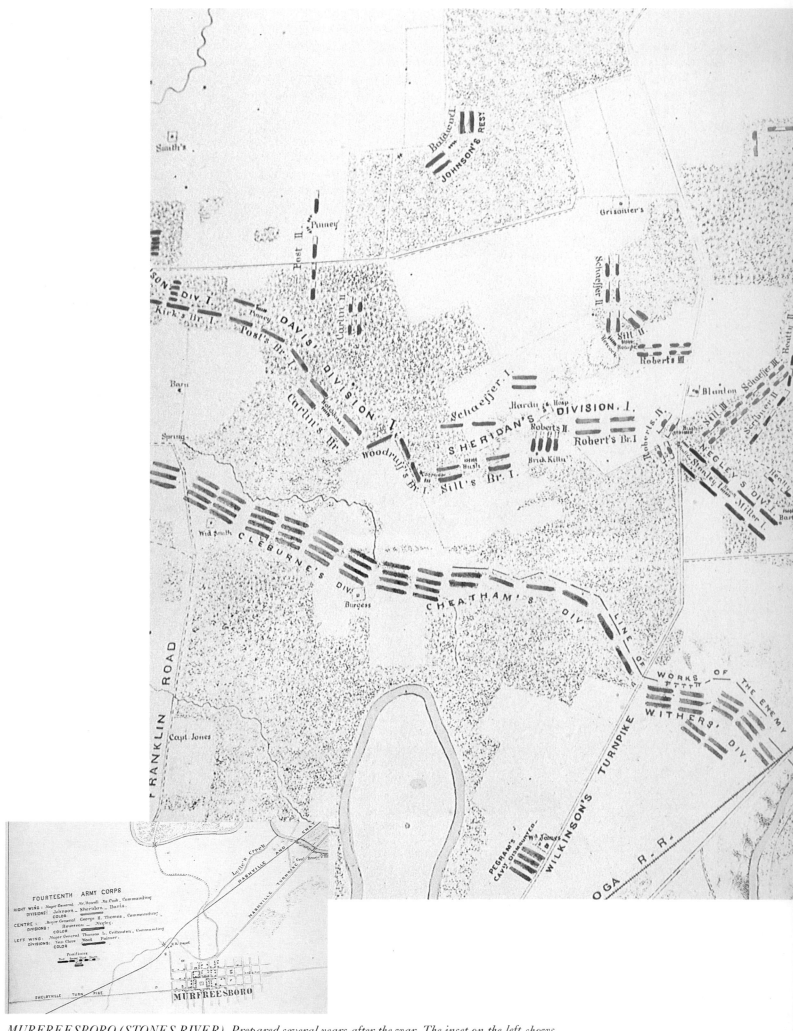

MURFREESBORO (STONES RIVER). Prepared several years after the war. The inset on the left shows the color coding; the right inset shows the alignment of the two armies during the bitter battle late in December, 1862.

CHANCELLORSVILLE

Second Day: May 2, 1863

CHANCELLORSVILLE: At first light on May 2 Jackson begins a flank march (lower right) across the Union front. Sickles glimpses the tail of this column, moves forward from Hazel Grove, and attacks (1). His minor success convinces Hooker that the Confederates are in full retreat, and that Lee's probing attacks (2) are merely rear-guard actions. Jackson, meanwhile, has gone into position athwart the Union right flank, which faces south along the Turnpike. At 6 P.M. he drives forward (3), routing the XI Corps, his wide battle line overlapping the desperate Union attempts to form (4). The victorious Confederates sweep up the Turnpike, past the Wilderness Church and Dowdall's Tavern. Here remnants of the XI Corps make a last stand (5) and, reinforced with a few guns, delay Jackson's men long enough for the rest of the troops to make good their escape. Sickles falls back to Hazel Grove, where Union guns knock back a Rebel attack (6) threatening this key position. The fire of Hooker's massed artillery at Fairview Cemetery (7) finally halts the Southern advance. At 9 P.M. Jackson and his staff, returning from a reconnoitering mission to locate the new Federal positions, are fired on by a nervous Confederate regiment, and Jackson is fatally wounded (8).

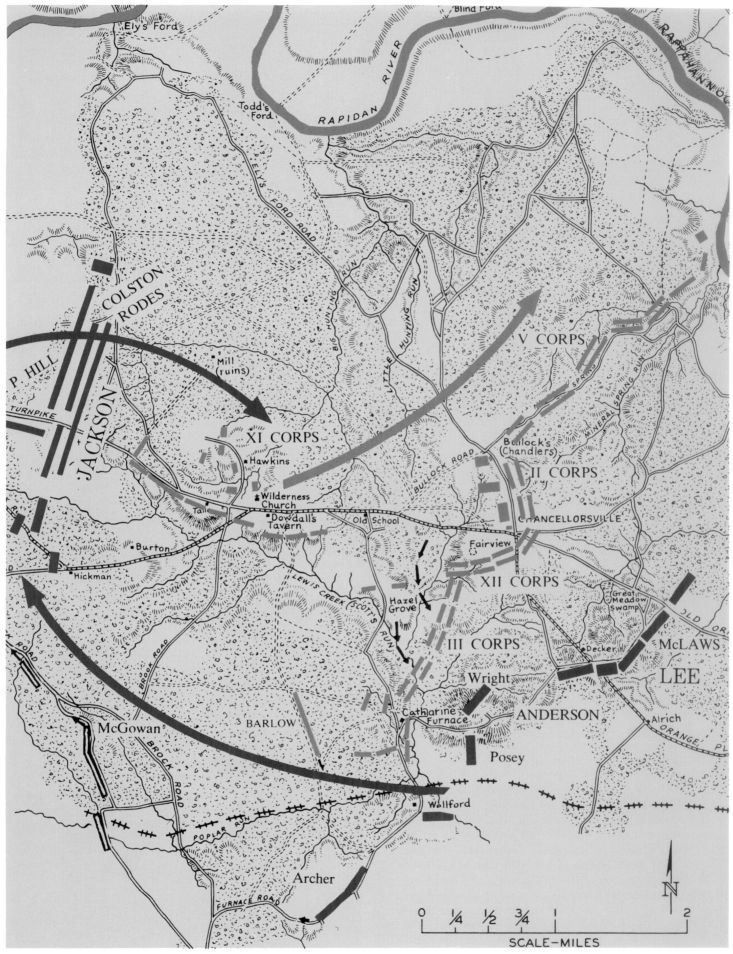

Map shows Jackson's flanking movement at 6 P.M., May 2, 1863.

54,000 men at Lee's rear. For all this, Hooker had failed to act decisively on the twenty-ninth. By pressing his three corps forward, he could have opened Banks's Ford and forced Lee back on the town of Fredericksburg and the Confederate positions. Once again, a Union general's timidity and indecision, under the guise of "awaiting developments and reinforcements," would prove disastrous.

Hooker remained inactive on April 30. Reinforced by Sickles's corps, he had almost 75,000 troops near Chancellorsville. In fairness to Hooker, however, the ground over which he was operating, a part of the "Wilderness," confined him almost exclusively to road movement and made it difficult to bring his superior numbers to bear on Lee's troops. Lee faced a difficult decision. Caught between Sedgwick's 40,000 troops at Fredericksburg and Hooker's other five corps, a less resolute commander would have stood on the defensive or withdrawn to a more secure position. But Lee, supported by Jackson, took the offensive.

A reconnaissance of Sedgwick's position convinced Lee that an attack on the Fredericksburg front would thrust his infantry into a strong position, well supported by artillery. Leaving a screening force of 10,000 men, under Early, Lee marched off to deal with Hooker's main army. Taking the divisions of Hill, Rodes, Colston, and McLaws, he moved first to the rear of Anderson's position, near Tabernacle Church. Anderson had begun building entrenchments, which stretched across the Or-

ange Plank Road and the Orange Turnpike. With the arrival of Jackson, on the morning of May 1, this work stopped, and 40,000 Confederates moved to the attack. Hooker had also put his command on the march at midmorning on May 1. Fierce but inconclusive fighting began between George Sykes's troops and McLaws's division. Forced back by the Confederates, Sykes's troops rallied around Winfield S. Hancock's position and stopped the Confederate advance.

Hooker now had three corps in the battle area: Meade's V Corps, moving unmolested around the Confederate right; Sickles's III Corps, in reserve; and Couch's II Corps, moving in the center. Having put his superior force in motion, Hooker's seemingly decisive demeanor collapsed. Unnerved by the aggressiveness of what he knew to be a less numerous Confederate force, he ordered his troops to withdraw to positions around Chancellorsville, placing his least reliable formation, XI Corps, under Howard, to protect the right flank. On the evening of May 1, Lee and Jackson held their last council of war. After a reconnaissance of the Union position, Lee sent Jackson with the cavalry and 26,000 infantry—well over half of the available troops—to circle the Union position and attack the exposed right flank. The stage was set for a brilliant Confederate victory and for the last joint maneuver of one of the most audacious combinations of military leadership to be seen in the nineteenth century—Lee and Jackson.

Left to right: Maj. Gen. Joseph Hooker, Maj. Gen. Oliver O. Howard, Gen. Robert E. Lee, Maj. Gen. Thomas J. Jackson

THE VICKSBURG CAMPAIGN

November 2, 1862–July 4, 1863

In the aftermath of the Battle of Shiloh, Henry Halleck assumed overall direction of the combined armies of Don Carlos Buell and U. S. Grant, numbering some 110.000 men in June,1862. In September, in order to meet Braxton Bragg's invasion of Kentucky, a portion of the army, under Buell's command, moved to that theater. Grant was left with 42,000 troops, with which he guarded the rail lines in western Tennessee and northern Mississippi.

On two separate occasions, in May and June of 1862, units of the Union navy had ascended the Mississippi River as far as Vicksburg, Mississippi, and attempted to force the Confederates to surrender the town. The first attempt found Union admiral David Farragut without an adequate landing force when the Confederates refused to surrender. A three days' bombardment on the second attempt also failed to break Southern resistance. However, Baton Rouge, Louisiana, was captured during this expedition, lost, then reoccupied for good in September 1862.

Those Confederate troops left behind by Bragg on his move into Kentucky totaled over 30,000 men, commanded by Sterling Price and Earl Van Dorn. By the end of September, those officers had determined to make a move on the Federal communications guarded by Grant's army. Confederate movements were disorganized, and Union countermoves were equally uncoordinated. The resulting battle, at Iuka, Mississippi, between Union troops under William S. Rosecrans and Confederate forces under Price, ended in a stalemate. Price then joined with Van Dorn and moved to attack the Union position at Corinth, Mississippi. Fierce fighting there resulted in a Union victory, with almost 4,800 Confederate casualties, compared with 3,100 for the Union. The Union forces initiated a slow pursuit, with the Confederates falling back to Holly Springs, Mississippi.

Grant at last obtained permission from Halleck to move against Vicksburg, beginning his march southward on November 2 with about 72,000 troops. Grant initially found himself unopposed by Van Dorn, who retreated from Holly Springs to Grenada, Mississippi. Grant reached Holly Springs on November 20. He continued his overland advance, but Van Dorn, with only 24,000 troops, began actively contesting it. Grant became intent on using the Union's naval superiority to his advantage and, on December 9, ordered William T. Sherman, with four divisions, back to Memphis, Tennessee, in order to proceed by boat to Vicksburg. To support Grant's overland campaign,

Nathaniel P. Banks would advance up the Mississippi from New Orleans.

Sherman left Memphis on December 20, the same day that Van Dorn's cavalry was attacking and destroying Grant's main base at Holly Springs. Sherman's four divisions arrived at Vicksburg on December 26. John C. Pemberton, the Confederate commander there, was feverishly concentrating troops to block Sherman; by December 27, Pemberton had assembled 12,000 men, opposing 32,000 Union troops. Sherman, wasting no time, attacked the Confederate positions at Chickasaw Bluffs, just north of Vicksburg, on December 29. The Confederates, entrenched and ready for the Union assault, repulsed it easily. Sherman's attempt to move upriver and attack at Haynes' Bluff also ended in failure, on December 31. He then withdrew to Milliken's Bend, and on January 2, 1863, he and his troops became part of John McClernand's corps. Banks moved only as far as Baton Rouge.

Grant, his communications threatened and without confidence in McClernand's abilities, decided to abandon his overland campaign, leaving Stephen A. Hurlbut's corps to guard the lines of communication. Grant began moving the balance of his army to the river at Vicksburg. While Grant was so engaged, McClernand moved his corps into Arkansas to capture the Confederate fort at Arkansas Post. In this he was successful, but Grant, considering this diversion of manpower unnecessary, ordered McClernand back to Milliken's Bend. Grant arrived there on January 29 and, the next day, assumed personal command of the overall campaign against Vicksburg.

Above: Aerial view showing the Mississippi River. Dot: Vicksburg.
Left: Eagle of the Eighth *by Don Troiani. The Eighth Wisconsin going into action at Vicksburg.*

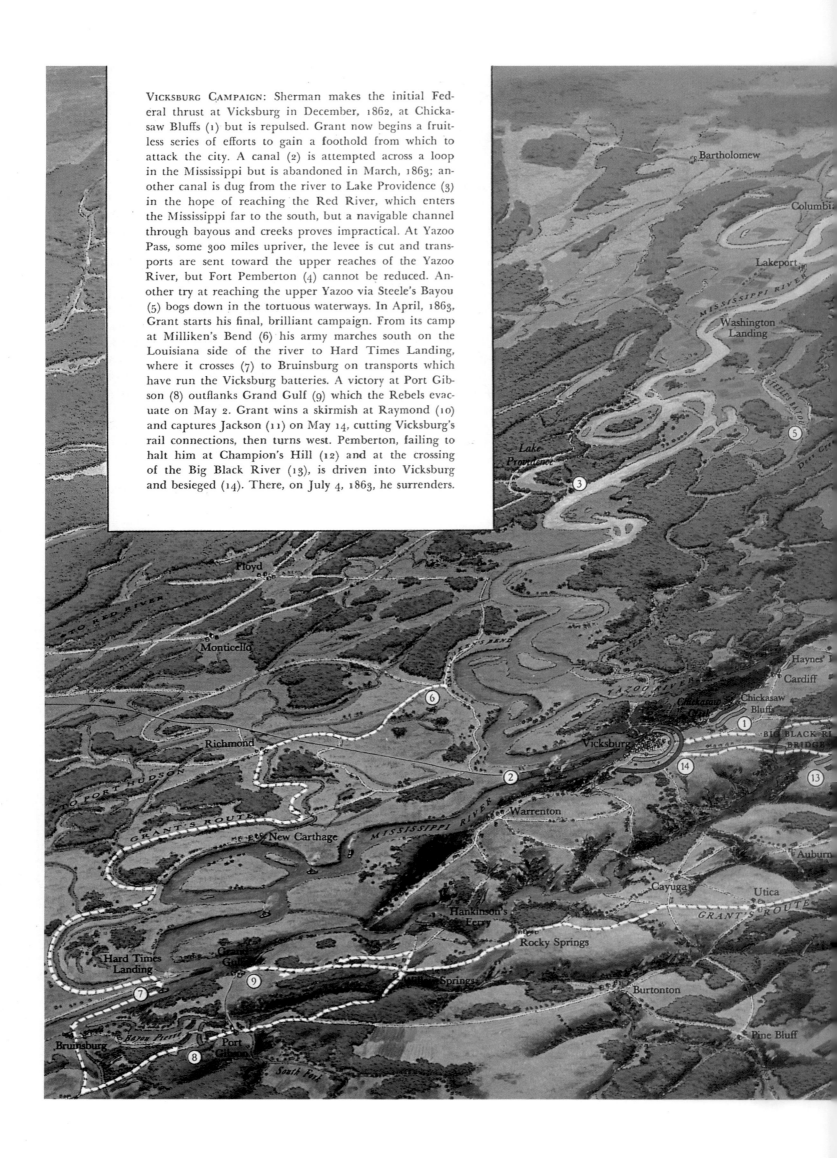

VICKSBURG CAMPAIGN: Sherman makes the initial Federal thrust at Vicksburg in December, 1862, at Chickasaw Bluffs (1) but is repulsed. Grant now begins a fruitless series of efforts to gain a foothold from which to attack the city. A canal (2) is attempted across a loop in the Mississippi but is abandoned in March, 1863; another canal is dug from the river to Lake Providence (3) in the hope of reaching the Red River, which enters the Mississippi far to the south, but a navigable channel through bayous and creeks proves impractical. At Yazoo Pass, some 300 miles upriver, the levee is cut and transports are sent toward the upper reaches of the Yazoo River, but Fort Pemberton (4) cannot be reduced. Another try at reaching the upper Yazoo via Steele's Bayou (5) bogs down in the tortuous waterways. In April, 1863, Grant starts his final, brilliant campaign. From its camp at Milliken's Bend (6) his army marches south on the Louisiana side of the river to Hard Times Landing, where it crosses (7) to Bruinsburg on transports which have run the Vicksburg batteries. A victory at Port Gibson (8) outflanks Grand Gulf (9) which the Rebels evacuate on May 2. Grant wins a skirmish at Raymond (10) and captures Jackson (11) on May 14, cutting Vicksburg's rail connections, then turns west. Pemberton, failing to halt him at Champion's Hill (12) and at the crossing of the Big Black River (13), is driven into Vicksburg and besieged (14). There, on July 4, 1863, he surrenders.

FORT PEMBERTON ④

Greenville

N

TO YAZOO PASS

YAZOO RIVER

LITTLE RIVER

SUNFLOWER RIVER

Benton

Yazoo City

YAZOO RIVER

Lincoln

Clairbornesville

Livingson

NUT HILLS

Mt. Olympus

Brownsville

Battle Springs

Bridgeport

VICKSBURG & JACKSON R.R.

Clinton

⑪

CHAMPION'S HILL

⑫

Jackson

Raymond

w Auburn

⑩

NEW ORLEANS & JACKSON R.R.

PEARL RIVER

Crystal Springs

THE CAMPAIGN
AND SIEGE OF VICKSBURG

December, 1862 – July, 1863

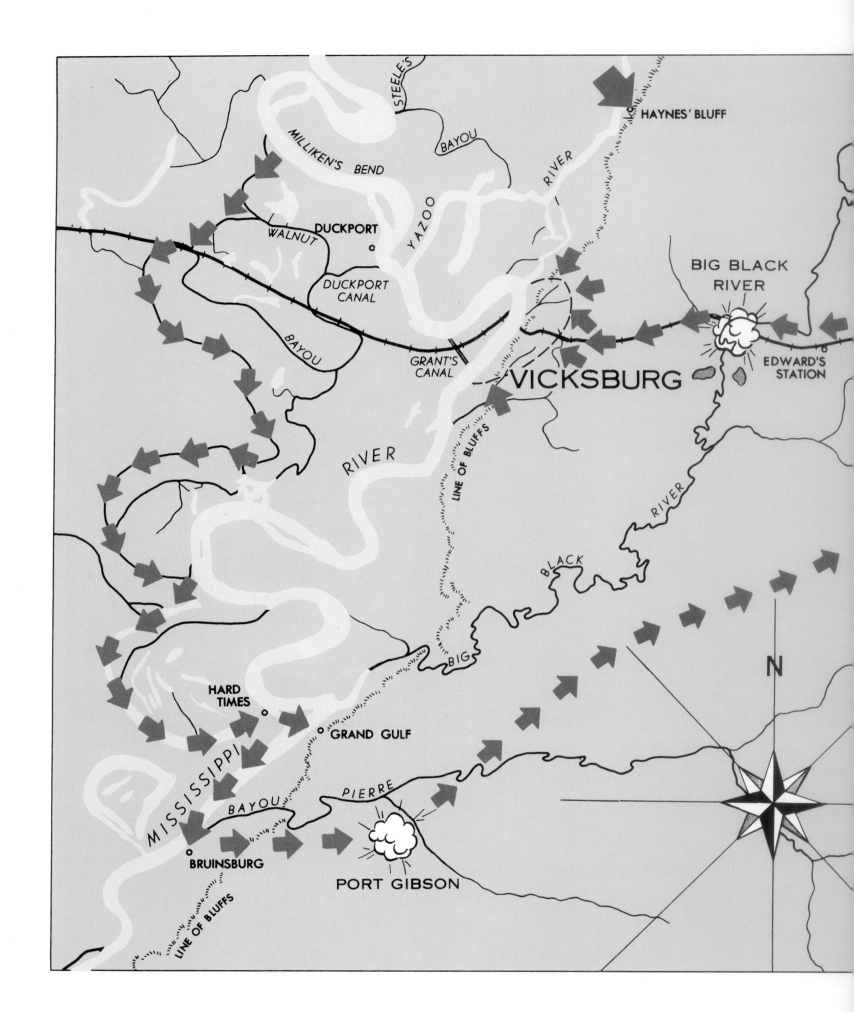

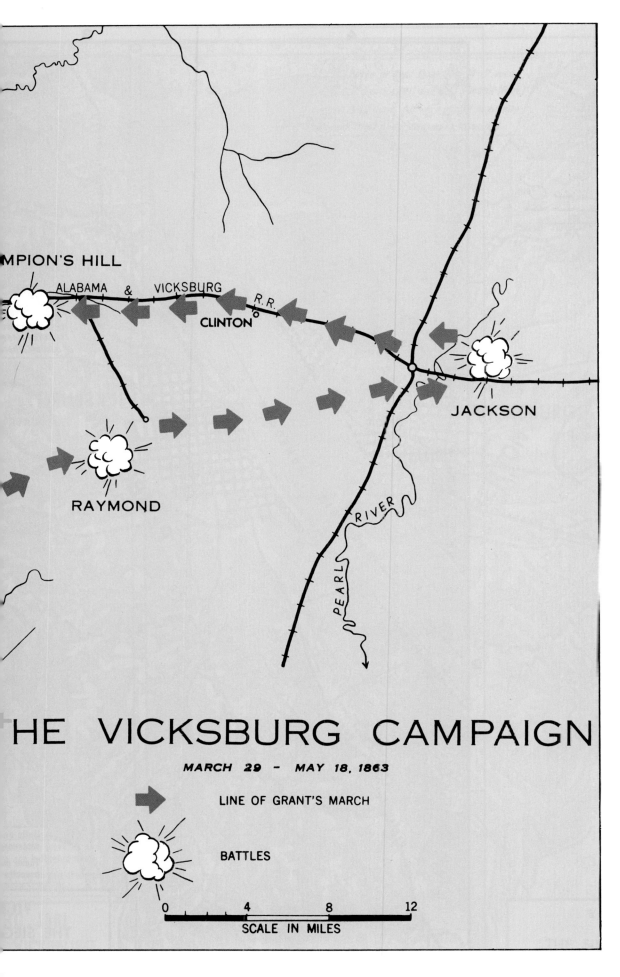

MPION'S HILL

ALABAMA & VICKSBURG

CLINTON

R.R.

JACKSON

RAYMOND

PEARL RIVER

HE VICKSBURG CAMPAIGN

MARCH 29 - MAY 18, 1863

LINE OF GRANT'S MARCH

BATTLES

0   4   8   12
SCALE IN MILES

Top to bottom: Maj. Gen. Ulysses S. Grant, Maj. Gen. Earl Van Dorn,
Lt. Gen. John C. Pemberton, Rear Adm. David D. Porter

THE BATTLE OF GETTYSBURG

July 1–3, 1863

The victory at Chancellorsville cost the Confederacy almost 13,000 casualties and the life of Stonewall Jackson. James Longstreet's return from southern Virginia and the reinforcement of the Army of Northern Virginia to over 75,000 troops required the Confederates to reorganize.

Jackson could not be replaced, but a decision to create three corps allowed for the promotion of Richard S. Ewell to command II Corps and A. P. Hill, III Corps. Six division commanders retained their commands: Lafayette McLaws, John B. Hood, George Pickett, Jubal Early, Robert E. Rodes, and R. H. Anderson. Three men, Henry Heth, Edward Johnson, and William D. Pender, were handling divisional responsibilities for the first time. The cavalry remained under Jeb Stuart.

Joseph Hooker was not relieved of command in the aftermath of Chancellorsville, and despite his troops having suffered more than 17,000 casualties, the Union army organization remained intact.

With the Confederate decision to invade the North, Robert E. Lee moved the corps of Longstreet and Ewell toward the Shenandoah Valley, leaving Hill to hold Fredericksburg, Virginia, and fool the Union forces into believing that Lee's entire army was still there. Alfred Pleasonton's attack on Stuart at Brandy Station, Virginia, on June 9 indicated a large body of Confederate infantry around Culpeper Court House. Hooker, reacting to this information, began shifting parts of the Army of the Potomac westward.

By June 17, the army was concentrated near Chantilly, Virginia, preparing to move toward Harpers Ferry. Ewell had crossed the Potomac River near Sharpsburg, Maryland, while Longstreet and Hill were moving down the Shenandoah Valley toward Harpers Ferry. Albert Jenkins's brigade of cavalry, detached from Stuart, had reached Fayetteville, Pennsylvania.

The Union army remained in northern Virginia until June 24. On that day, Hooker started out for Frederick, Maryland. Ewell's corps had by this time reached Chambersburg, Pennsylvania, and Longstreet was near Hagerstown, Maryland, with Hill's men also marching there. Stuart's cavalry, less four brigades, which were with Lee's main body, continued to protect the Blue Ridge Mountain gaps from Pleasonton's troopers. Stuart's reduced strength prevented him from gathering much intelligence on Union movements.

June 27 found most of the Union troops near Frederick and

Aerial view of Gettysburg and the battlefield to the south of the town. Dot: Gettysburg.

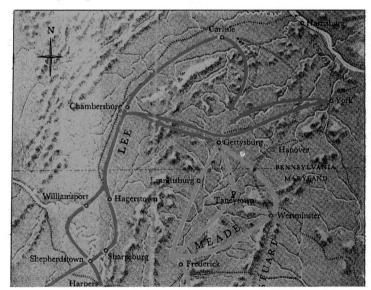

Lee's army was spread over 100 miles at one point in his invasion of Pennsylvania. Prior to concentrating at Gettysburg, some of his advance units were as far east as the Susquehanna River. Confederate-red, Union-blue
Left: Fight for Colors by Don Troiani.

GETTYSBURG

Second Day: July 2, 1863

Gettysburg

SEMINARY RIDGE

ZIEGLER'S GROVE

CODORI HOUSE

ROGERS HOUSE

MEADE'S HQ

CEMETERY HILL

CULP'S HILL

CEMETERY RIDGE

TROSTLE FARM

PEACH ORCHARD

WHEAT FIELD

WARFIELD HOUSE

EMMITSBURG ROAD

ROSE HOUSE

7

8

6

5

3

David Greenspan

GETTYSBURG: The action on the second day opens with a Confederate artillery barrage at 4 P.M. An hour later Hood's Rebel division sweeps in around the Union left flank, overruns Devil's Den (1), and begins the ascent of the undefended Little Round Top, which dominates the entire Federal position. Warren hastens troops to the crest, and they repulse Hood's men after a bitter struggle (2). As the battle shifts steadily northward, Longstreet sends in Mc-Laws, who shatters Sickles' salient (3), embracing the Peach Orchard and the Wheat Field, and advances toward a gap in Meade's line (4). Artillery is rushed forward to hold together the battered Union line until reinforcements arrive. At the Trostle Farm, Barksdale's Mississippians manage to take a Yankee battery (5), but Barksdale is mortally wounded and his brigade wrecked. The Rebels strike at the Union center (6), where they meet stiff resistance, including a doomed counterattack by the 1st Minnesota, and are stopped. At dark Ewell demonstrates against the Federal right, but fails to take the strong position on Culp's Hill (7). In the day's final action Jubal Early gets two Rebel brigades in among the Union batteries on Cemetery Hill (8), but they are not strong enough to resist counterattacks and are driven off.

Middletown, Maryland. Union cavalry units were directed to Emmitsburg, Maryland, and Gettysburg, Pennsylvania. At this point, Lee was unaware of Hooker's dispositions.

Although Hooker had maneuvered his units well, there was uncertainty in Washington, D.C., regarding his combat readiness as an army commander. This was understandable in view of his inadequacies at Chancellorsville. Hooker, despite large reinforcements, had contracted "McClellan's Syndrome" and believed himself badly outnumbered by Lee. Hooker's reluctance to leave a garrison at Maryland Heights, astride Lee's line of communication, worsened his relations with President Lincoln and Henry Halleck, and Hooker's request to be relieved was acted upon in the early hours of June 28. George G. Meade, elevated from command of V Corps (where he was replaced by George Sykes), would command the Union army in one of its most crucial battles, a battle that was to begin fewer than seventy-two hours later.

By the night of Meade's first day of command, the Confederates were spread out over southern Pennsylvania. Longstreet was at Chambersburg, with Hill nearby in the town of Greenwood. Two of Ewell's divisions, those of Rodes and Johnson, were at Carlisle. Early's division, less John B. Gordon's brigade, was at York. Gordon's men had advanced to the banks of the Susquehanna River at Wrightsville. Stuart's cavalry, now riding at the rear of the Union army and crossing the Potomac near Washington, was effectively out of the campaign. The Confederates had briefly skirmished with various portions of the Pennsylvania militia but had not encountered any serious resistance. Foraging conditions were excellent and morale was high. With Stuart's cavalry away, Lee had limited information on Union intentions. On June 28, a spy reporting to Longstreet placed the Union army at Frederick, Maryland, with Meade in command. At 4:00 A.M., Meade had his army on the march.

Lee decided to concentrate his forces at Cashtown, Pennsylvania, about halfway between Gettysburg and Chambersburg. By June 30, only Heth's division was there, but most of the infantry was within a day's march. The cavalry was still scattered, with Stuart's main body near Hanover, Pennsylvania, and only Jenkins's and John Imboden's brigades within supporting distance of Lee. Meade's seven corps were strung out along the Pennsylvania-Maryland border, with John F. Reynolds's I Corps and Henry Slocum's XII Corps actually in Pennsylvania. Oliver O. Howard's XI Corps and Daniel Sickles's III Corps were near

Emmitsburg, Maryland. The balance of the army was gathered at points just north of Westminster.

John Buford's cavalry division was in Gettysburg, screening the approaches west of town. With no up-to-date information on Union troop whereabouts, Hill agreed to a request from Heth to take his division to Gettysburg in search of shoes. Heth, followed by Pender's troops, left Cashtown at 5:00 A.M. on July 1. Approaching Gettysburg at about 8:00 A.M., Heth's men encountered Buford's outposts, and sharp fighting began. By 10:00 A.M., the Union troopers had been forced out of position, but they had held on long enough to allow elements of Reynolds's I Corps to reach the battlefield. Reynolds was killed, and his corps was taken over by Abner Doubleday. Early afternoon found Heth and Pender locked in combat with I Corps. Rodes's and Early's divisions, arriving from north of the town, attacked two divisions of the newly arrived XI Corps (now under Carl Schurz, with Howard in overall command of Union forces on the field) and began driving them back into Gettysburg. By 6:00 P.M., the Union troops had been forced back through Gettysburg, taking up positions on Cemetery Hill and Culp's Hill, and along Cemetery Ridge. Reinforced by divisions from XII Corps and III Corps, with Winfield S. Hancock in command, the Union forces frantically tried to improve their defensive positions. Anderson's and Johnson's divisions had arrived on the Confederate side, and the fighting of the first day had gone heavily in their favor.

Lee planned to assault both ends of the Union lines the next day. However, unforeseen delays prevented the Confederates from attacking until late in the afternoon, reducing the chances of success, as Union reinforcements kept pouring in all through the morning and afternoon. Failing to drive the Union forces from their positions on July 2, Lee determined on a single, narrow frontal attack by 15,000 troops directly at the center of the Union defenses on Cemetery Ridge. Against the advice of Longstreet, he launched portions of Pender's, Heth's, and Anderson's divisions, plus the whole of Pickett's division, against the strength of the Union position. The attacking force was shot to pieces, with numerous men captured. Lee held his ground on July 4 and contemplated his casualties, which were estimated at 20,000 to 28,000 men. The Union forces suffered 23,000 casualties. Both sides were exhausted after three days of heavy fighting, and Meade's army only halfheartedly pursued Lee's tattered troops. These, in turn, were able to escape over the swollen Potomac River at Williamsport, Pennsylvania.

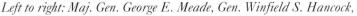

Left to right: Maj. Gen. George E. Meade, Gen. Winfield S. Hancock,   *Gen. John Reynolds,*   *Maj. Gen. Lafayette McLaws,*   *Maj. Ge*

George Pickett

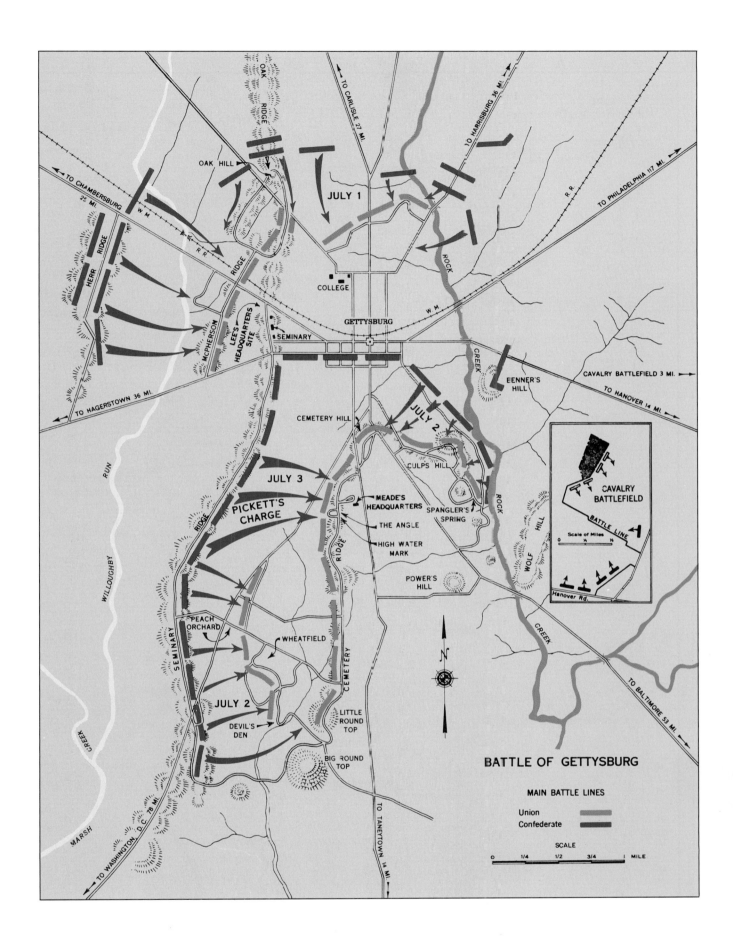

TO CARLISLE 27 MI.

TO HARRISBURG 36 MI.

OAK RIDGE

OAK HILL

TO CHAMBERSBURG 25 MI.

JULY 1

TO PHILADELPHIA 117 MI.

HERR RIDGE

W.M.

RIDGE

R.R.

COLLEGE

ROCK

W.M.

McPHERSON

LEE'S HEADQUARTERS SITE

GETTYSBURG

SEMINARY

TO HAGERSTOWN 36 MI.

EENNER'S HILL

CAVALRY BATTLEFIELD 3 MI.

TO HANOVER 14 MI.

CEMETERY HILL

CREEK

JULY 2

CULPS HILL

JULY 3

PICKETT'S CHARGE

MEADE'S HEADQUARTERS

SPANGLER'S SPRING

ROCK

THE ANGLE

HIGH WATER MARK

RIDGE

WOLF HILL

CAVALRY BATTLEFIELD

RUN

RIDGE

POWER'S HILL

BATTLE LINE

Scale of Miles

WILLOUGHBY

PEACH ORCHARD

WHEATFIELD

CEMETERY

Hanover Rd.

SEMINARY

N

JULY 2

LITTLE ROUND TOP

DEVIL'S DEN

TO WASHINGTON, D.C. 78 MI.

BIG ROUND TOP

CREEK

TO BALTIMORE 53 MI.

BATTLE OF GETTYSBURG

MARSH

MAIN BATTLE LINES

Union

Confederate

SCALE

0   1/4   1/2   3/4   1 MILE

TO TANEYTOWN 14 MI.

109

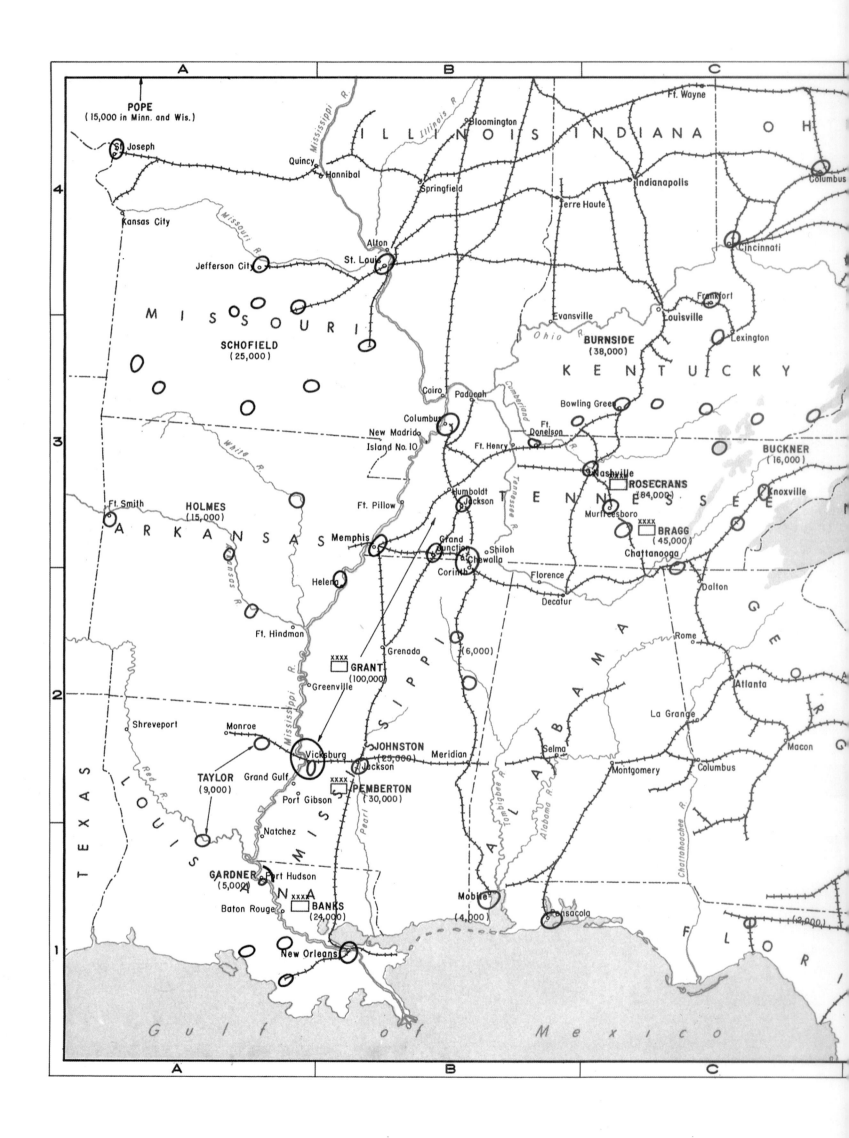

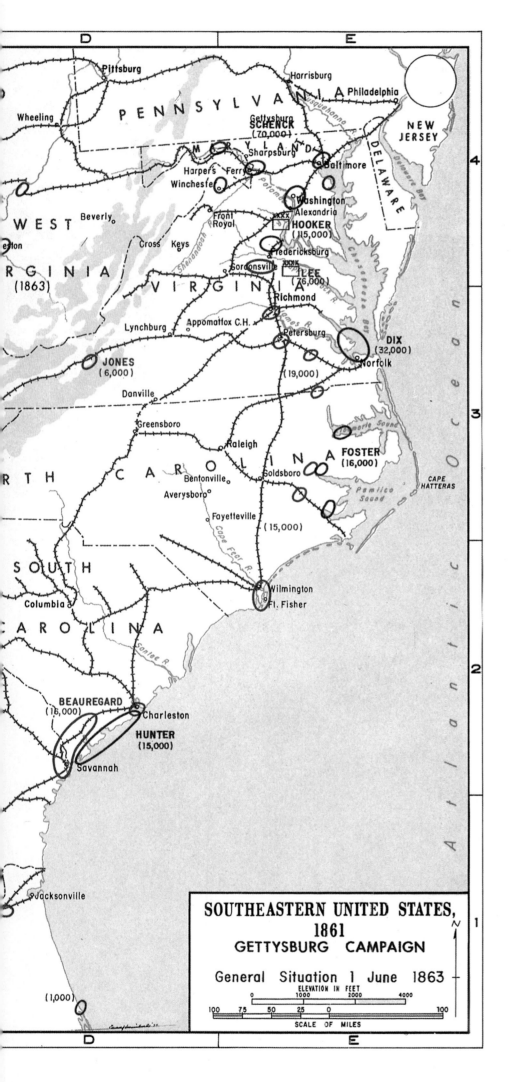

SOUTHEASTERN UNITED STATES, 1861
GETTYSBURG CAMPAIGN

General Situation 1 June 1863

N

ELEVATION IN FEET

1000 — 2000 — 4000

100 75 50 25 0   100

SCALE OF MILES

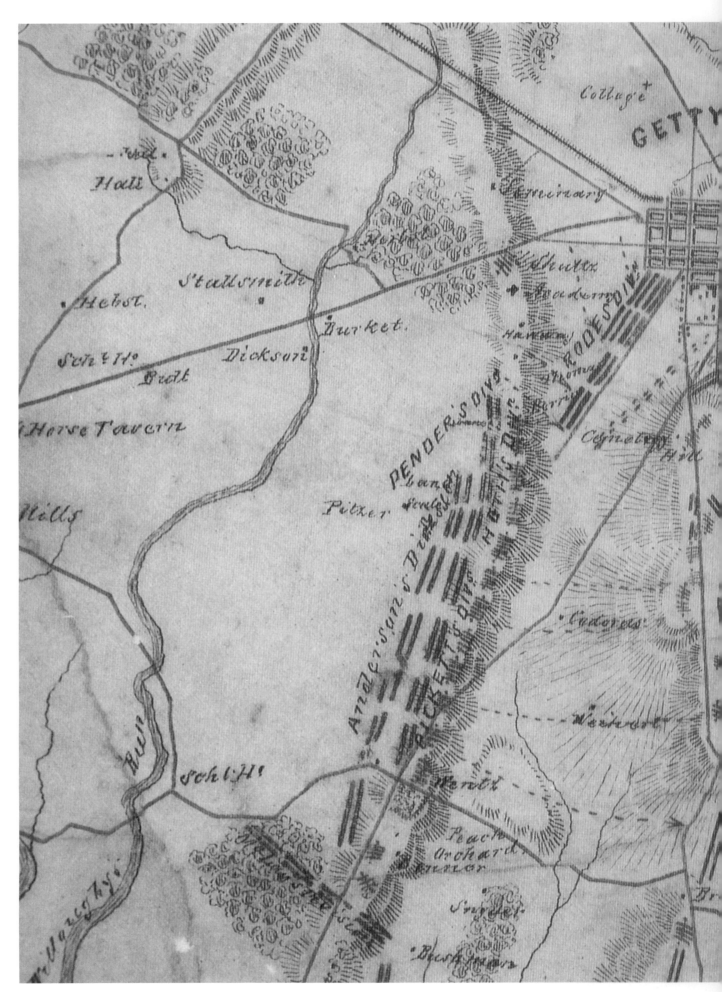

GETTYSBURG. Previously unpublished, parchment map, prepared by Confederate general J. F. Gilmer, chief of engineers, showing the battle positions for July 3, 1863.

The Gray Wall *by Don Troiani.*

THE BATTLE OF CHICKAMAUGA

September 19–20, 1863

After the Battle of Murfreesboro, Braxton Bragg and the Army of Tennessee retreated to strong defensive positions near Shelbyville and Wartrace, Tennessee. As William S. Rosecrans's Army of the Cumberland built up its strength, Bragg, in contrast, found his army dwindling as more and more Confederate resources were drawn into the struggle for Vicksburg, Mississippi.

Bragg's main goal was to protect Chattanooga, Tennessee, arguably the most important railroad junction in the Confederacy. Through Chattanooga passed the most nearly direct east–west rail line in the South. The Union commanders recognized this also, and Henry Halleck urged Rosecrans to advance against the city during the winter of 1862–63. But to no avail.

After a period of raiding each other's communications, Rosecrans finally decided to move against Bragg. On June 26, his army—now numbering some 56,000 infantry of four corps and 9,000 cavalry of one corps—began the advance from Murfreesboro, Tennessee

Bragg's army consisted of two corps of infantry, under William J. Hardee and Leonidas Polk, and one of cavalry, under Joseph Wheeler. There was a total of 30,000 infantry and 14,000 cavalry.

Rosecrans, intending to maneuver Bragg out of position, sent his cavalry, under David S. Stanley, and the reserve corps, under Gordon Granger, in a feint around Bragg's left flank at Shelbyville. His remaining infantry corps (XX Corps, under Alexander M. McCook; XXI Corps, under Thomas L. Crittenden; and XIV Corps, under George H. Thomas) would make a difficult march through Liberty Gap and Hoover's Gap in an attempt to turn the Confederate right.

By June 30, Rosecrans had forced Bragg back to Tullahoma, Tennessee, and Rosecrans occupied Manchester, Tennessee. Moving quickly to capture the crossings over the Elk River at Bragg's rear, Rosecrans forced the Confederates to retreat from Tullahoma. Bragg decided not to make a stand to the north of Chattanooga, and by July 4, he had retreated to a point south of the city. The "Tullahoma Campaign" was a major success for the Union's Army of the Cumberland.

Bragg then placed Polk's corps in Chattanooga in order to improve its defenses. Hardee's corps was placed astride the rail line to Knoxville, Tennessee. The cavalry was spread out, picketing the Tennessee River above and below Chattanooga. Rosecrans had halted his pursuit well before arriving at the river.

He resumed his advance when he crossed the river south of Chattanooga. Under cover of an excellent cavalry screen and a demonstration before the city by three brigades, Rosecrans's army crossed at Caperton's Ferry, Alabama, catching Bragg unawares. The crossing began on August 20 and was completed by September 4. Bragg then realized that a major battle was imminent. The divisions of W. H. T. Walker and Simon B. Buckner were ordered to join Bragg's army, and on September 7, James Longstreet's corps was detached from Lee's army in Virginia and sent west to join Bragg.

Bragg began his evacuation of Chattanooga on September 8, concentrating his army at La Fayette, Georgia. Rosecrans, victimized by the confusing roads, then made his first serious error of the campaign. Crittenden's corps marched by one road to Chattanooga; Thomas's, by another to Trenton, Georgia; and McCook's, by another to Valley Head, Alabama, on its way to Alpine, Georgia, on the Georgia-Alabama border. Thinking that Bragg was retreating in haste, Rosecrans urged his various corps to use utmost speed. The numerous routes they used separated them and rendered them incapable of supporting one another.

Above: Aerial view of Chickamauga battlefield.
Dot: Battlefield Park

CHICKAMAUGA

Second Day: September 20, 1863

KELLY HOUSE

POE HOUSE

BROTHERTON HOUSE

THOMAS' HQ

SNODGRASS HILL

SNODGRASS HOUSE

TO ROSSVILLE AND CHATTANOOGA

David Greenspan

BRAGG'S HQ

LAFAYETTE ROAD

VINIARD HOUSE

ROSECRANS HQ

OSBUR... HOUSE

JACKSON HOUSE

WITHERS HOUSE

DYER HOUSE

DRY VALLEY ROAD

VILLETOE HOUSE

West Chickam...

CHICKAMAUGA: At dawn on September 20 Rosecrans' Federal line roughly parallels the Lafayette Road, with Thomas holding a salient on the left at the Kelly House. The second day's battle starts at 9 A.M., when Bragg sends Polk's wing against Thomas' breastworks (1); Thomas repulses the heavy assaults. Wood's division pulls out of line to go to Thomas' aid, leaving a hole in the Union center. At this moment, shortly before noon, Longstreet charges with the Confederate left wing, breaking through the gap between the Brotherton and Viniard houses (2). The Federal right is crushed and flees in disorder (3); swept along with it are Rosecrans and two of his three corps commanders, Crittenden and McCook. Longstreet now turns north and hits Thomas' lightly defended flank (4) on Snodgrass Hill. Thomas patches up a line, standing firm and earning his sobriquet, "The Rock of Chickamauga." Longstreet is sliding toward Thomas' rear when Granger, on his own initiative, orders Steedman's division from the Union reserve to the front. Steedman's arrival (5) checks Longstreet's turning movement about 2:30 P.M. Thomas continues to repel stiff Rebel attacks the rest of the afternoon, then joins the retreat to Rossville and Chattanooga at sundown. Bragg permits the Federal army to escape to safety.

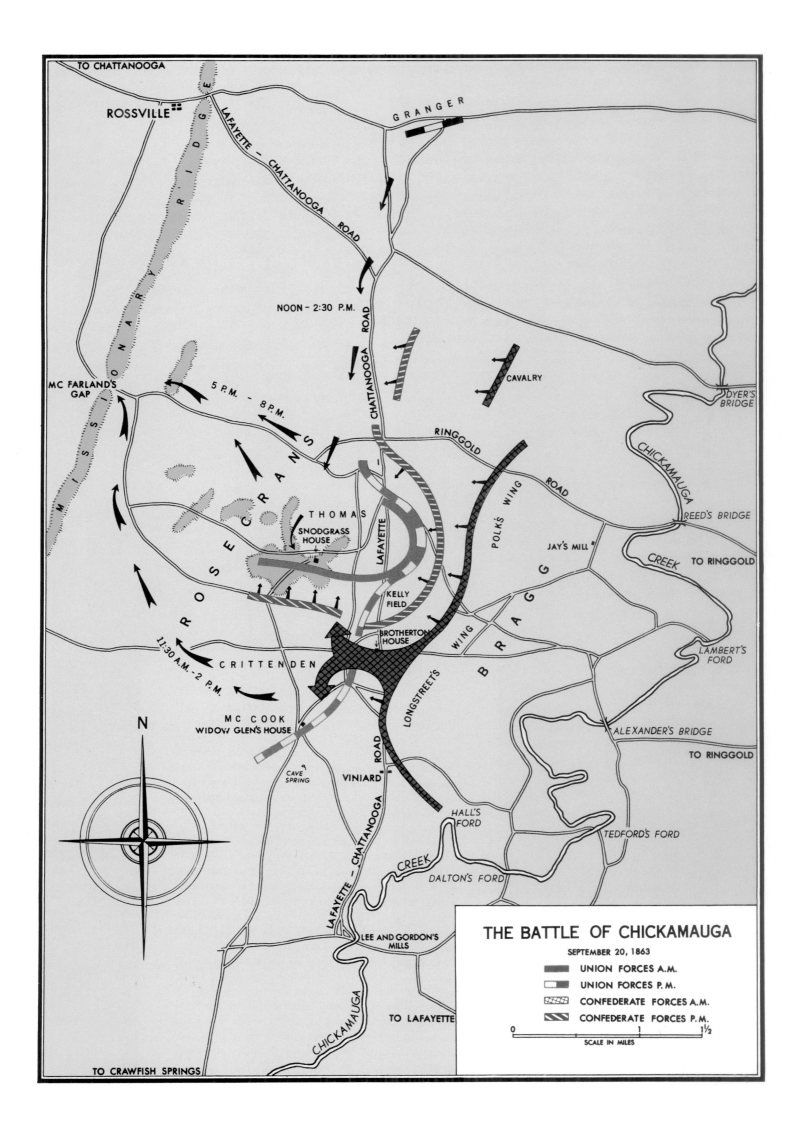

TO CHATTANOOGA

ROSSVILLE

GRANGER

MISSIONARY RIDGE

LAFAYETTE - CHATTANOOGA ROAD

NOON - 2:30 P.M.

MC FARLAND'S GAP

CHATTANOOGA ROAD

CAVALRY

DYER'S BRIDGE

5 P.M. - 8 P.M.

CHICKAMAUGA

RINGGOLD

REED'S BRIDGE

R O S E C R A N S

THOMAS

SNODGRASS HOUSE

LAFAYETTE

POLK'S WING ROAD

JAY'S MILL

CREEK

TO RINGGOLD

KELLY FIELD

11:30 A.M. - 2 P.M.

CRITTENDEN

BROTHERTON HOUSE

WING

LONGSTREET'S WING

B R A G G

LAMBERT'S FORD

MC COOK

WIDOW GLEN'S HOUSE

CAVE SPRING

VINIARD

CHATTANOOGA ROAD

ALEXANDER'S BRIDGE

TO RINGGOLD

N

HALL'S FORD

TEDFORD'S FORD

LAFAYETTE - CHATTANOOGA ROAD

CREEK

DALTON'S FORD

LEE AND GORDON'S MILLS

CHICKAMAUGA

TO LAFAYETTE

TO CRAWFISH SPRINGS

THE BATTLE OF CHICKAMAUGA

SEPTEMBER 20, 1863

UNION FORCES A.M.
UNION FORCES P.M.
CONFEDERATE FORCES A.M.
CONFEDERATE FORCES P.M.

0   1   1½

SCALE IN MILES

By September 12, Crittenden's troops were moving south from Chattanooga, Thomas's men were at Stevens's Gap in Lookout Mountain, and McCook's divisions were at Alpine. Bragg's four corps were dispersed from La Fayette (occupied by D. H. Hill's corps), across Pigeon Mountain (the corps of Walker and Buckner), to Lee and Gordon's Mills. There Polk's infantry and Nathan Bedford Forrest's cavalry corps faced Crittenden's men across a narrow stream called Chickamauga Creek. Wheeler and Stanley opposed each other south of La Fayette.

Bragg's initial attempt to crush Crittenden's corps foundered on Polk's caution and on his own ineffective troop dispositions. However, despite Rosecrans's efforts to close up his army, the Union forces remained scattered. September 17 found Crittenden at Lee and Gordon's Mills; Granger at Rossville, Georgia, some ten miles in the rear; Thomas at Pond Spring (over five miles from Crittenden); and McCook at Stevens's Gap (over five miles from Thomas).

In effective contrast, Bragg had his army concentrated opposite Lee and Gordon's Mills, with Forrest's and Wheeler's cavalry screening the flanks. Bragg aggressively determined to make the attack on Crittenden. With several of Longstreet's brigades arriving on September 18, and with more due the following day, Bragg set his army in motion. By dawn on September 19, he had the bulk of his army (47,500 infantry and 14,500 cavalry) on the west bank of Chickamauga Creek, facing Crittenden's corps (14,000), with Thomas (23,000) in reserve. Granger's reserve corps (6,000) was also within supporting distance.

The Confederates first engaged John M. Brannan's division, sent forward by Thomas to attack what he thought was only a Confederate brigade. His men encountered Forrest's cavalry, and a fierce fight ensued. Thomas's corps was heavily engaged and reinforced by Crittenden and a portion of McCook's command. Bragg deployed the bulk of his army, having succeeded in getting all of it west of Chickamauga Creek.

He decided to renew the attack as early as possible on September 20. During the night, more of Longstreet's men arrived from Virginia as reinforcements. The second day would see some of the fiercest fighting experienced by either army, with a final casualty list of over 16,000 Union troops and 18,400 Confederate.

Major Gen. William S. Rosecrans

Major Gen. George H. Thomas

Major Gen. Thomas L. Crittenden

Major Gen. Braxton Bragg

Major Gen. James Longstreet

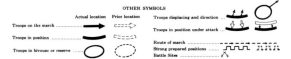

TABLE OF SYMBOLS

BASIC SYMBOLS

Regiment	 III	Infantry	⊠
Brigade	 X	Cavalry	⊘
Division	 XX	Cavalry Covering Force	• • • • • •
Corps	 XXX	Artillery	⊡
Army	 XXXX	Artillery In Position	⊞⊞⊞
		(Does not indicate type or quantity)	
		Trains	☐

EXAMPLES OF COMBINATIONS OF BASIC SYMBOLS

Barksdale's Infantry Brigade
of McLaws' Division .... ⊠ Barksdale (McLaws)

Stuart's Cavalry Division .... ⊘ Stuart (−)
Minus Detachments

First Corps .... ⊡⊡⊡

Rosecrans' Army
of the Cumberland XXXX
                              CUMBERLAND ROSECRANS

OTHER SYMBOLS

	Actual location	Prior location	
Troops on the march	➡	⇨	
Troops in position	◖	◌	
Troops in bivouac or reserve	◯	◌	

Troops displacing and direction ...

Troops in position under attack ...

Route of march .... ▭▭▭▭▭ ΛΛΛ

Strong prepared positions ....

Battle Sites .... ⚔

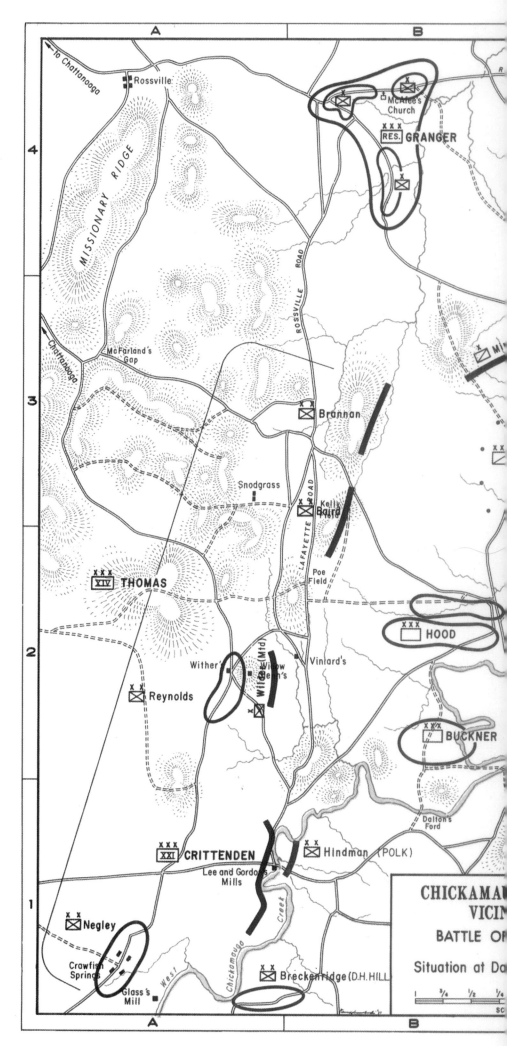

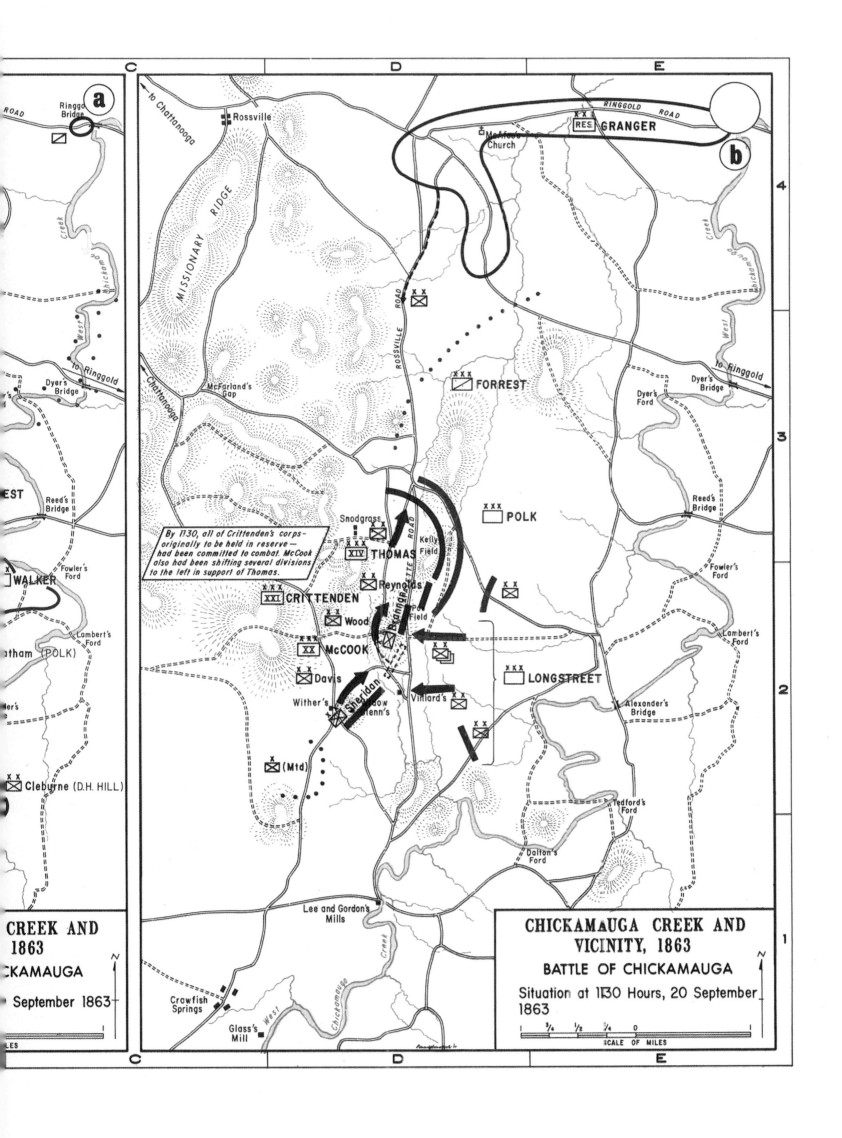

a

Ringgo
Bridge

to Chattanooga

Rossville

MISSIONARY RIDGE

Chattanooga

RINGGOLD ROAD

RES GRANGER

McAfee's
Church

b

to Ringgold

Dyer's
Bridge

McFarland's
Gap

ROSSVILLE ROAD

XXX FORREST

Dyer's
Ford

Dyer's
Bridge

Reed's
Bridge

Snodgrass

By 1130, all of Crittenden's corps—
originally to be held in reserve—
had been committed to combat. McCook
also had been shifting several divisions
to the left in support of Thomas.

XIV THOMAS

Kelly
Field

XXX POLK

Reed's
Bridge

WALKER

Fowler's
Ford

Reynolds

CRITTENDEN

Po Field

Fowler's
Ford

XXX

Lambert's
Ford

tham (POLK)

Wood

BRANNAN ROAD

McCOOK

LONGSTREET

Lambert's
Ford

Davis

Alexander's
Bridge

Wither's

Sheridan
Widow
Glenn's

Vinlard's

Cleburne (D.H. HILL)

(Mtd)

Tedford's
Ford

Dalton's
Ford

Lee and Gordon's
Mills

CREEK AND
1863

CKAMAUGA

September 1863

N

LES

Crawfish
Springs

Glass's
Mill

West

Chickamauga

Creek

N

**CHICKAMAUGA CREEK AND
VICINITY, 1863**

BATTLE OF CHICKAMAUGA

Situation at 1130 Hours, 20 September
1863

3/4   1/2   3/4   0   1
SCALE OF MILES

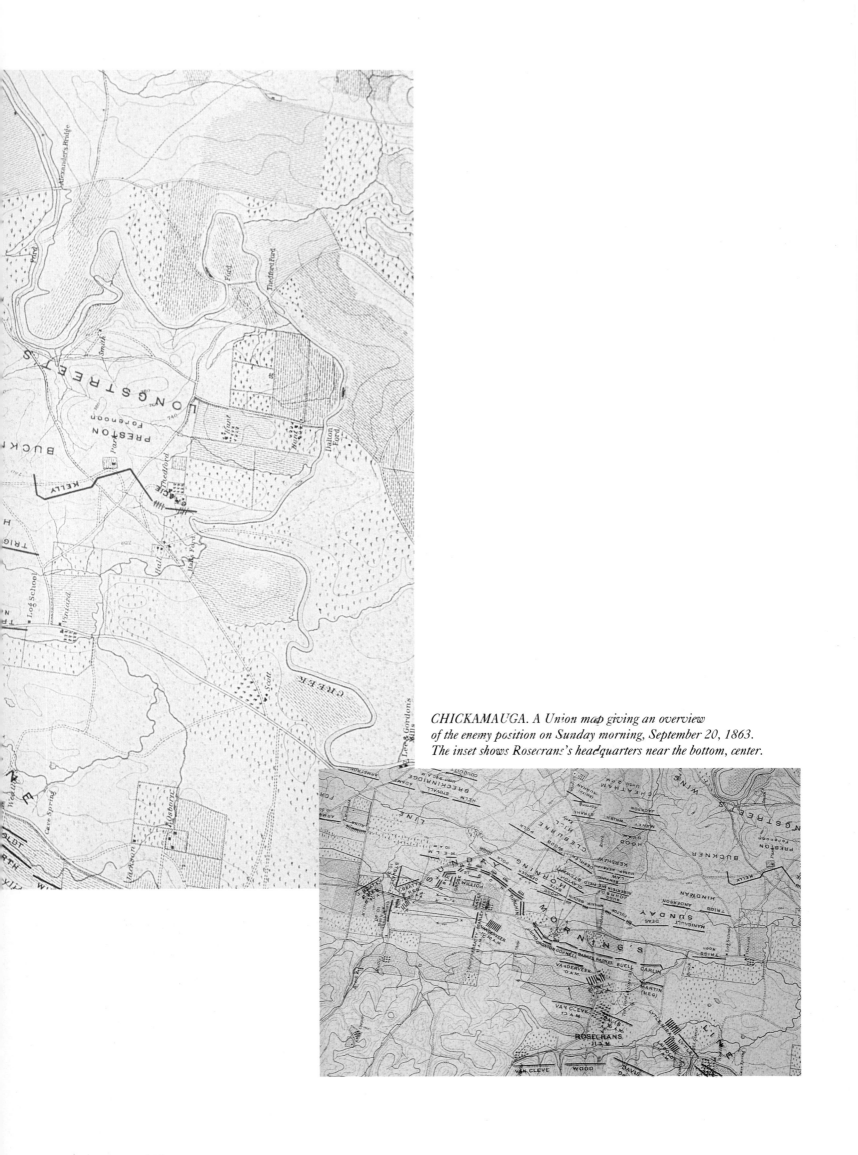

*CHICKAMAUGA. A Union map giving an overview
of the enemy position on Sunday morning, September 20, 1863.
The inset shows Rosecrans's headquarters near the bottom, center.*

THE BATTLE FOR CHATTANOOGA

November 23–25, 1863

Staggered by casualties, which approached 30 percent for both armies, the Union forces abandoned the field at Chickamauga and retreated into Chattanooga, Tennessee. William S. Rosecrans, having lost his ability to maneuver—the source of much of his success against Braxton Bragg— resigned himself to a Confederate siege. Bragg arrived at Chattanooga by nightfall, September 21. With the Confederates dominating the high ground around the city (Missionary Ridge, Lookout Mountain, and Orchard Knob), the Union supply situation became acute. Rosecrans was forced to supply his army by a circuitous route, one that crossed the Tennessee River by pontoon bridge. The railroad and direct roads into Chattanooga from Bridgeport, Alabama, the hub of Rosecrans's logistics system, were controlled by the Confederates.

Bragg, hypnotized by the paralysis that had beset Rosecrans, ignored moves that might have given the Confederates quick control of the city, such as crossing the river above or below Chattanooga, thus gaining the Union rear. Instead, Bragg decided on the least aggressive course, a siege of the city.

Bragg sent Joseph Wheeler's cavalry off to raid Rosecrans's communications. This raid, lasting from October 1 to October 8, was unsuccessful, and Wheeler was fortunate to extricate his command from the north side of the Tennessee River.

By October 27, however, the strain on the lengthy Union supply line had reduced the number of available horses and wagons, so that the troops in Chattanooga were on greatly diminished rations. Fearful of the consequences of the loss of Chattanooga, Henry Halleck decided to send reinforcements. Joseph Hooker, with XI Corps and XII Corps from the Army of the Potomac, arrived at Nashville, Tennessee, on October 4, and the troops were placed on duty guarding the rail lines.

U. S. Grant, put in overall command of Union troops in this theater in mid-October, was given a choice of retaining Rosecrans or placing George H. Thomas in command of the Army of the Cumberland. He selected Thomas, who took over on October 19.

Grant arrived in Chattanooga on October 23, and Union morale rose. Other changes had taken place in the Union command structure: Gordon Granger now commanded the consolidated old corps of Thomas L. Crittenden and Alexander M. McCook (now called IV Corps); and John M. Palmer was given command of XIV Corps.

The Confederates had made some changes of their own. After his success at Chickamauga, Bragg had managed to alienate some of his better officers, and as a consequence, D. H. Hill, Leonidas Polk, and Simon B. Buckner had left the Army of Tennessee for other commands. Bragg's three remaining corps were commanded by James Longstreet, William J. Hardee, and John C. Breckinridge.

But for one notable event, October would have ended with little more than the constant skirmishing and occasional artillery shelling that had heretofore characterized the siege of Chattanooga. Thomas, daring a risky amphibious maneuver, succeeded in opening the direct supply route from Bridgeport through Wauhatchie, Tennessee, and, thence, into Chattanooga. Union troops, under William B. Hazen, supported by Hooker's men from Bridgeport, crossed the Tennessee River near Brown's Ferry and surprised the Confederate brigade at Wauhatchie, commanded by Evander Law. The withdrawal of Law and the Confederate cavalry on October 27 opened the short, direct supply route, and by the next day, it was in operation. A Confed-

Above: Aerial view of the city of Chattanooga and the Tennessee River. Dot: Chattanooga
Left: Cleburne's Men *by Don Troiani, showing the distinct blue & white unit flag of General Patrick Cleburne.*

The Federal Army of the Cumberland was besieged within the fortifications of Chattanooga (1) when Grant arrived on October 23, 1863, over an inadequate, almost impassable road across the mountains to the north of the river. Braxton Bragg's Confederate Army of Tennessee, on Missionary Ridge (foreground) and Lookout Mountain (left), completely dominated the Federal lines. On the twenty-seventh the Federals pried open a route, dubbed "the cracker line," to their supply depots at Bridgeport via Brown's Ferry (2). Less than a month later Grant took the offensive. On November 23, George Thomas' Army of the Cumberland seized Orchard Knob (3), high ground in the plain before Missionary Ridge. The next day General Joseph Hooker stormed up Lookout Mountain (4) to threaten Bragg's left flank. At the same time, Sherman crossed the Tennessee (5), but his misdirected attack struck too far north (6). On November 25, Sherman having made no progress against Pat Cleburne's division in the area of the tunnel (7) on the Confederate right, Grant ordered Thomas to apply pressure on Bragg's center. The Army of the Cumberland overran the Confederate positions at the base of Missionary Ridge (8); after a pause for breath, the Yankees drove on up the slope and over the crest of the ridge (9), forcing the Confederates to flee in confusion.

MAP: DAVID GREENSPAN

RAISING THE SIEGE OF
CHATTANOOGA

Orchard Knob: November 23, 1863
Lookout Mountain: November 24, 1863
Missionary Ridge: November 25, 1863

Left to right: Major Gen. Ulysses S. Grant, Major Gen. William T. Sherman, Major Gen. Braxton Bragg,   Gen. William J. Hardee

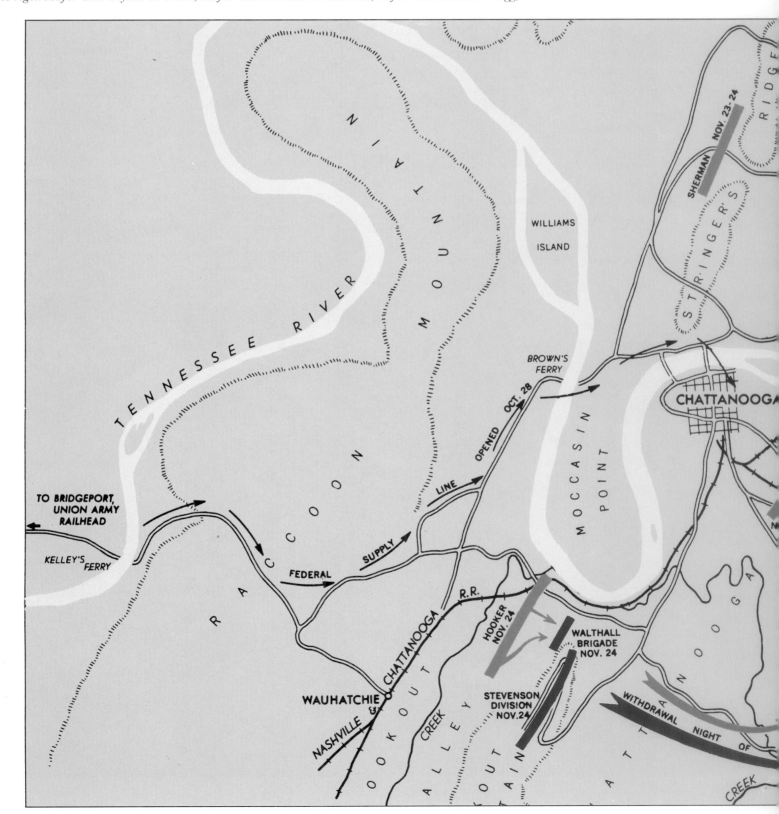

erate night attack on October 28–29, aimed at disrupting the new route, ended in failure.

More Union reinforcements—XV Corps and XVII Corps, under William T. Sherman—arrived at Bridgeport on November 15. With Longstreet's corps having been detached to operate against Ambrose Burnside at Knoxville, Tennessee, Bragg was now greatly weakened. In order to relieve the pressure on Knoxville and give himself more room for maneuver at Chattanooga, Grant prepared to attack. Moving Sherman across the Tennessee River and above the city, opposite Tunnel Hill, and skillfully deploying Thomas's troops, Grant set the stage for lifting the siege. The assault on Orchard Knob on November 23 began a series of battles that resulted in the near total collapse of the Confederate Army of Tennessee.

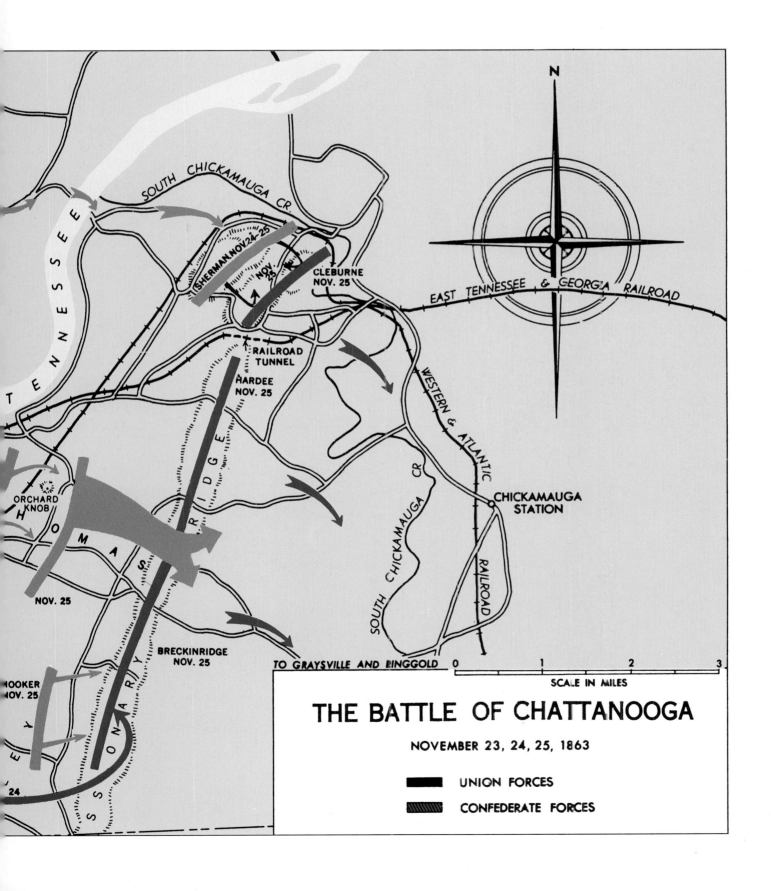

THE BATTLE OF CHATTANOOGA

NOVEMBER 23, 24, 25, 1863

UNION FORCES

CONFEDERATE FORCES

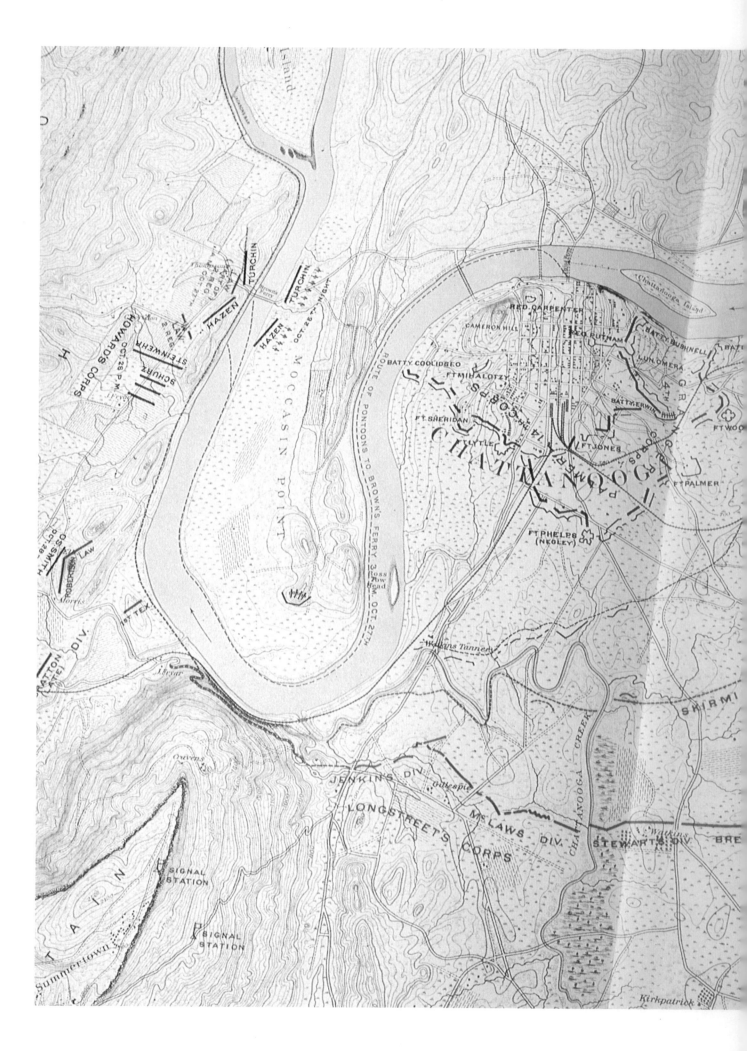

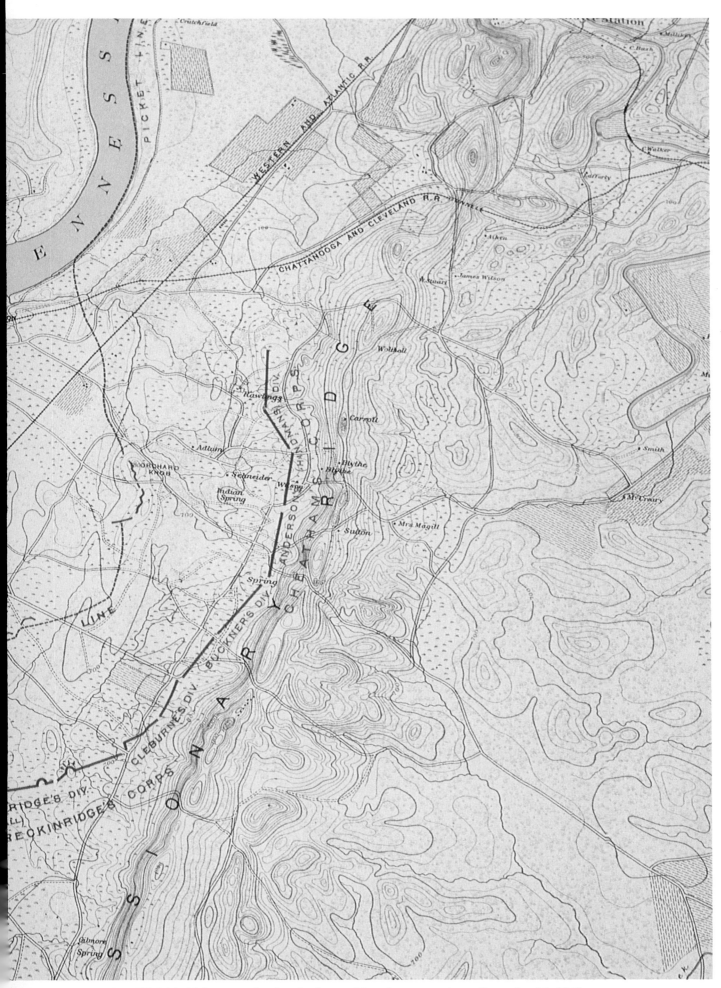

CHATTANOOGA. Union map showing the siege positions for two armies on September 24, 1863.

THE BATTLES OF THE WILDERNESS AND SPOTSYLVANIA

May 5–21, 1864

In the spring of 1864, the Confederacy was on the defensive in both the east and the west. U. S. Grant had moved to Virginia to coordinate overall Union strategy and direct, as necessary, George G. Meade's Army of the Potomac. William T. Sherman commanded the Union army in the western theater and was prepared to move on Atlanta, Georgia, in cooperation with Grant's campaign in Virginia.

With the exception of some inconclusive fighting at Bristoe Station and Rappahannock Station, as well as along Mine Run, the winter of 1863–64 in Virginia had been largely uneventful. Despite the fact that Robert E. Lee had been weakened badly in September by the reinforcement of Braxton Bragg's troops by James Longstreet's I Corps, Meade had failed to exploit his advantage in numbers. The Mine Run campaign concluded on December 1, 1863, and the armies went into winter quarters. Meade's unspectacular generalship had played a part in Grant's transfer to Virginia.

Both sides wanted to put their armies in the best possible situation for the spring campaign of 1864. The Army of the Potomac was reorganized yet again, this time into four infantry corps (II under Winfield S. Hancock, V under Gouverneur K. Warren, VI under John Sedgwick, and IX under Ambrose Burnside) and a cavalry corps under Philip Sheridan. By the time the campaign started, Meade's army numbered almost 119,000 men, including 12,000 cavalry. The recall of Longstreet's corps from east Tennessee reunited the Army of Northern Virginia.

Lee maintained the same organization as at Gettysburg, but now his army mustered only 64,000 troops, including Jeb Stuart's 8,400 sabers. Lee placed the corps of Richard S. Ewell and A. P. Hill in strong positions behind the Rapidan River, with Stuart picketing the Rappahannock River south to Fredericksburg, Virginia. Longstreet's corps was in reserve near Gordonsville, Virginia. The Union corps of Warren, Sedgwick, and Hancock were aligned north of the Rapidan, with Burnside's IX Corps guarding the Orange and Alexandria Railroad from Manassas Junction to Rappahannock Station. Sheridan's cavalry was picketing the front of the Union army.

Grant realized that Lee's position along the Rapidan was too strong to be assaulted, so Grant decided to turn Lee's position by crossing at Germanna Ford and Ely's Ford, downriver toward Fredericksburg. To this end, Grant mobilized the army on May 3. The next day, Lee recognized Grant's intentions and began moving his troops to counter them. The Union plan involved a certain amount of risk. The Union infantry columns, using a poor road network, would be passing across the front of the Confederate line of advance, exposing the Union flanks. Late on May 4, Hancock's II Corps, having crossed at Ely's Ford, reached Chancellorsville, Virginia. Warren's V Corps, with Sedgwick's VI Corps following, crossed at Germanna Ford and was bivouacked around Wilderness Tavern, astride the Orange–Fredericksburg Turnpike. Burnside, following Sedgwick, had yet to cross the Rapidan. Ewell's line of march was down the turnpike, and II Corps, bivouacked at Locust Grove and unbeknownst to Warren, was less than five miles from his position. Hill's III Corps (less R. H. Anderson's division) was advancing down the Orange Plank Road toward Chancellorsville. Longstreet, having the greatest distance to cover, was still en route from Gordonsville, Virginia.

On the morning of May 5, Ewell's advance blundered into Warren's marching men. Poor cavalry work had left both sides in the dark about the others' whereabouts. Lee had not wanted to

Aerial view of the Wilderness and Spotsylvania battlefields. Dot: Battlefield Park.
Left: Dead Confederate soldier on the battlefield.

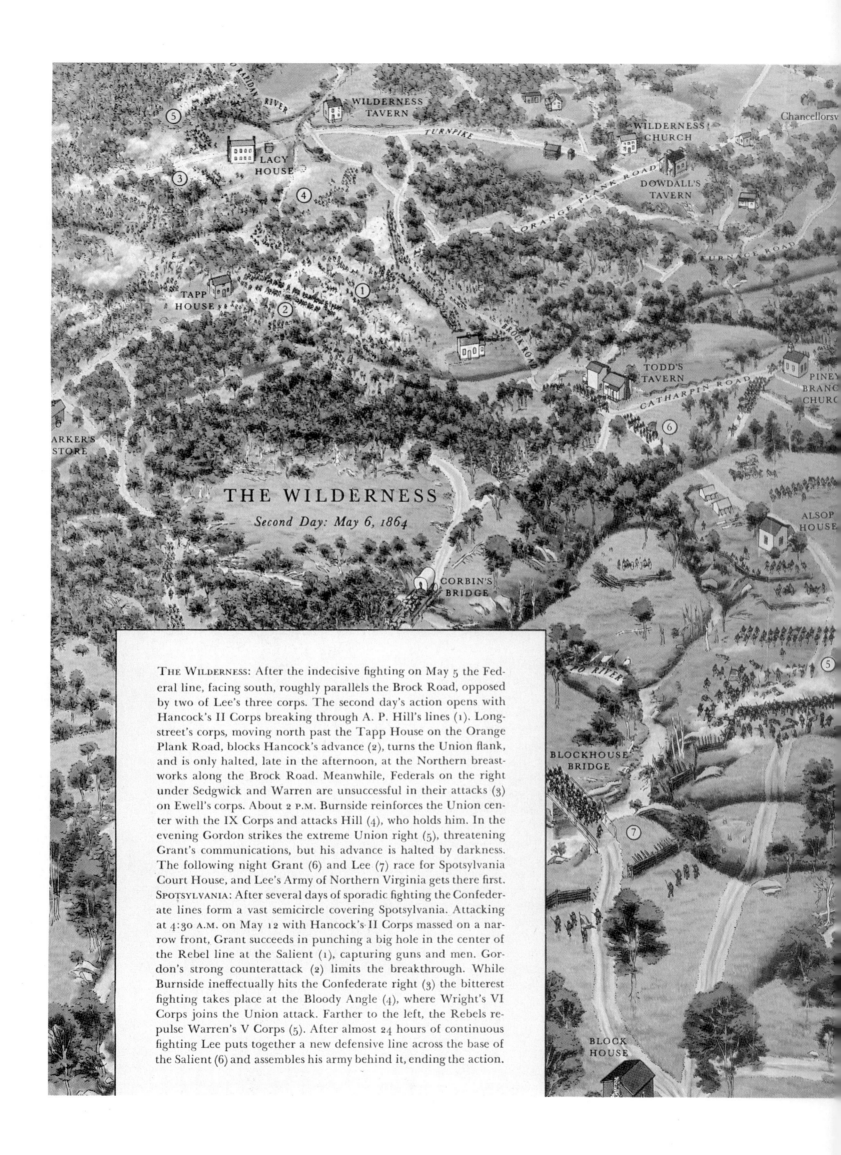

THE WILDERNESS

Second Day: May 6, 1864

THE WILDERNESS: After the indecisive fighting on May 5 the Federal line, facing south, roughly parallels the Brock Road, opposed by two of Lee's three corps. The second day's action opens with Hancock's II Corps breaking through A. P. Hill's lines (1). Longstreet's corps, moving north past the Tapp House on the Orange Plank Road, blocks Hancock's advance (2), turns the Union flank, and is only halted, late in the afternoon, at the Northern breastworks along the Brock Road. Meanwhile, Federals on the right under Sedgwick and Warren are unsuccessful in their attacks (3) on Ewell's corps. About 2 P.M. Burnside reinforces the Union center with the IX Corps and attacks Hill (4), who holds him. In the evening Gordon strikes the extreme Union right (5), threatening Grant's communications, but his advance is halted by darkness. The following night Grant (6) and Lee (7) race for Spotsylvania Court House, and Lee's Army of Northern Virginia gets there first.

SPOTSYLVANIA: After several days of sporadic fighting the Confederate lines form a vast semicircle covering Spotsylvania. Attacking at 4:30 A.M. on May 12 with Hancock's II Corps massed on a narrow front, Grant succeeds in punching a big hole in the center of the Rebel line at the Salient (1), capturing guns and men. Gordon's strong counterattack (2) limits the breakthrough. While Burnside ineffectually hits the Confederate right (3) the bitterest fighting takes place at the Bloody Angle (4), where Wright's VI Corps joins the Union attack. Farther to the left, the Rebels repulse Warren's V Corps (5). After almost 24 hours of continuous fighting Lee puts together a new defensive line across the base of the Salient (6) and assembles his army behind it, ending the action.

SPOTSYLVANIA

Fourth Day: May 12, 1864

TURNPIKE

ORANGE PLANK ROAD

UNFINISHED RAILROAD

SALEM CHURCH

N

LANDRUM HOUSE

NY RIVER

SALIENT

④

①

③

BLOODY ANGLE

McCOOL HOUSE

②

HARRISON HOUSE

BROCK ROAD

⑥

TO SPOTSYLVANIA C.H.

do battle without Longstreet, but the fight between Ewell and Warren started in earnest, as Hancock began moving toward Todd's Tavern. Sedgwick would guard Warren's flank as he attacked Ewell.

The late afternoon of May 5 found Ewell's 17,000 men locked in combat with 36,000 of Warren's and Sedgwick's infantry corps. Only the dense woods and lack of roads kept Ewell from being overrun. Hill's men on the Plank Road came up on Ewell's right and encountered a portion of Hancock's corps. Hill formed a line near the Tapp House, and late in the day was attacked by Hancock. Fierce fighting in both sectors was terminated by nightfall. Lines were consolidated as both sides awaited reinforcements: Longstreet's corps and Anderson's division (of Hill's corps) on the Confederate side and Burnside's corps on the Union.

At first light on the morning of May 6, the Union army again went over to the attack, Sedgwick and Warren assaulting Ewell's line, and Hancock renewing his battle with Hill's exhausted divisions. Ewell's veterans, backed by artillery, repulsed the Union onslaught. Hancock, however, had enough troops to overlap Hill's line at each end. Heavily outnumbered and outflanked, the divisions of Henry Heth and Cadmus Wilcox were on the verge of being routed from the field. At this critical juncture, Longstreet arrived with his corps, trailed by Anderson's men. Longstreet accurately assessed the situation, and his counterattack (led by his adjutant, Colonel Gilbert M. Sorrel) blunted Hancock's assault, routed the Union men, and restored the line Hill's men had fought so savagely to hold. In the afternoon following this attack, Longstreet was gravely wounded by his own troops.

With the fighting in the Wilderness resulting in a stalemate, the evening of the following day (May 7), Grant began a movement to the east and south, hoping to turn Lee's right and place himself between the Confederates and Richmond, Virginia. A key road junction at Spotsylvania Court House became the critical point, and the Confederate army narrowly won the race. The battle for Spotsylvania began on May 8. Lee built a series of fortifications around the court house, which Grant determined to break by direct assault. The heaviest attacks came on May 10 and 12, and although a portion of the Confederate line was broken and overrun, Lee held his position and skillfully maneuvered his army to match a series of southeasterly movements by Grant. By May 21, Grant decided to abandon his attempts on Spotsylvania Court House and began moving his army toward the crossings of the North Anna River.

For several days, the Confederates successfully defended the crossings of the North Anna near Hanover Junction, Virginia, but Grant continued his strategy of attempting to maneuver around Lee's right. Finally, after crossing the Pamunkey River below Hanover Court House, Grant arrived near Cold Harbor, Virginia, on June 1.

Lee had again anticipated the Union movements, and had his army erecting earthworks to cover the approaches to Richmond, a scant ten miles from Cold Harbor. Grant again attempted to break the Confederate line with a major assault on June 3 and suffered 7,000 casualties.

Realizing his inability to dislodge the Southern army from its fortifications, Grant decided to outflank Lee by using his amphibious capabilities. An abortive attempt by Benjamin F. Butler to capture Petersburg, Virginia, had resulted in his army's being bottled up at Bermuda Hundred, Virginia, by Confederate troops under Pierre G. T. Beauregard. With the bulk of both armies still north of the James River, Grant determined to send William F. Smith's XVIII Corps by boat down the York River and up the James River to Petersburg, hoping that this force, in conjunction with Butler's men, might overwhelm Beauregard's

Previously unpublished photo of an unidentified group of Union soldiers, including an officer, lower right, and a drummer, far left.

small force before the Army of Northern Virginia could march to its relief.

Smith's men landed at Bermuda Hundred on June 14 and moved against Petersburg the following day. The balance of the Union army was also on the move, and for a period of time Lee was unaware of the seriousness of the Union threat. However, Beauregard fought a skillful delaying action against Smith and Butler until reinforcements could reach him. Grant was able to gain a numerical superiority opposite Petersburg, and he had the bulk of his army in position for an assault on June 18. The divisions of Charles W. Field and Joseph B. Kershaw, part of Longstreet's corps, arrived just before the attack and aided Beauregard in saving Petersburg, although a fair portion of the Confederates' outer defense positions fell to the Union troops. With the arrival of the bulk of Lee's army on June 19, Grant concluded he would have to begin siege operations.

The siege, lasting until August 2, was marked by heavy fighting, including the so-called Battle of the Crater, on July 30, 1864, and skillful use of entrenchments and interior lines by the Confederates. The war of attrition, however, began to go against the Confederates, and the Union superiority in manpower allowed Grant to stretch his lines south and west in an attempt to cut the railroads leading into Petersburg. With the breaking of the lines on August 2 and the Confederate defeat at Five Forks, Virginia, Lee decided to abandon both Petersburg and Richmond and march south to join Joseph E. Johnston's army, then around Smithfield, North Carolina.

Lee's weakened and ill-supplied army was no match for the Union cavalry under Philip Sheridan, and the infantry, sensing victory, simply outmarched the retreating Confederates, blocking their route to join Johnston. Finally, the Army of Northern Virginia was forced to acknowledge that the unequal struggle was over.

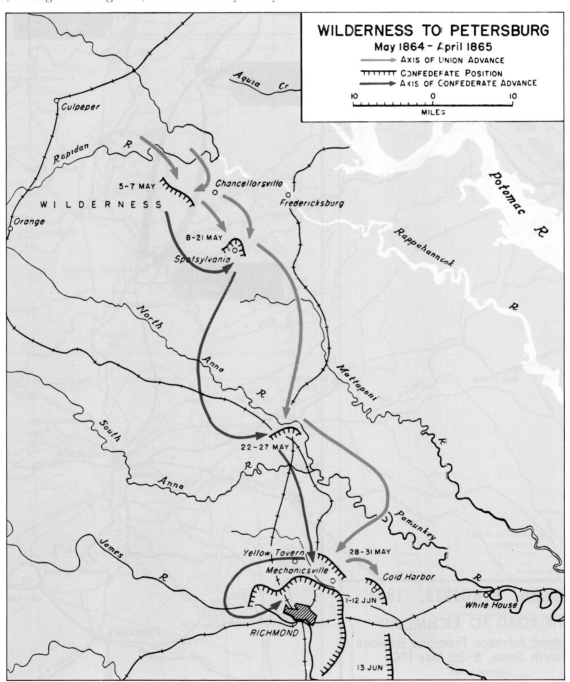

ATLANTA CAMPAIGN TO NASHVILLE

May 6–September 2, 1864

William T. Sherman's campaign against Atlanta was timed to coincide with U. S. Grant's movement against Lee in Virginia. On the morning of May 7, 1864, Sherman's three armies, under George H. Thomas, John M. Schofield, and James B. McPherson, began a southward movement from positions east and south of Chattanooga, Tennessee, toward the Confederate positions in front of Dalton, Georgia. The Confederate Army of Tennessee, under Joseph E. Johnston, was organized into two army corps under John B. Hood and William J. Hardee. A third, under Leonidas Polk, joined Johnston just after the opening of the campaign, bringing his strength to about 62,000. Standing on the defensive, Johnston might be expected to hold his ground against Sherman's 100,000 troops.

Sherman maneuvered Johnston out of his initial position at Dalton, assaulted the Confederate line at Resaca with little result, and, with the exception of a bloody assault at Kennesaw Mountain on June 27, outflanked Johnston and forced him out of successive positions without a major battle. A planned counterattack by the Confederates at Cassville, Georgia, on May 18 miscarried, and Johnston's constant retrograde movements caused the Confederate War Department and especially President Jefferson Davis, to lose faith in his ability to save Atlanta from the Union armies.

On July 17, 1864, with his back to Atlanta, and while drafting a plan to take the offensive, Johnston was relieved of command. His replacement, Hood, understood that his mandate was to fight for every foot of ground around Atlanta, and this he proceeded to do. On July 20, he sent two corps, Hardee's and Alexander P. Stewart's (formerly commanded by Polk, who had been killed on June 14), to assault the Union corps of Thomas's Army of the Cumberland, which was then crossing Peachtree Creek, barely five miles from Atlanta. Despite some early Confederate success, Thomas repulsed the attack.

July 22 found Atlanta enveloped on two sides by the Union army, the Confederates having been withdrawn into the entrenchments that ringed the city. Leaving Stewart's and Benjamin Cheatham's corps (formerly Hood's) to hold the city, Hood attempted to turn the Union left flank with Hardee's corps and Joseph Wheeler's cavalry. McPherson's Army of the Tennessee was under the mistaken impression that the Confederates were retreating and that a night march on July 21–22 had put Hardee well onto McPherson's flank and rear. The fighting that ensued

was at first favorable to the Confederates, resulting in the death of McPherson and the disorganization of his command. However, the Confederates were finally halted after some initial gains, and repulsed with heavy losses. On July 28 at Ezra Church, a subsequent attack on McPherson's command, now under Oliver O. Howard, was also beaten back.

After trading some cavalry raids with Hood in early and middle August, Sherman determined to wheel south of Atlanta and cut Hood's rail communications. This he was able to do by the end of August, despite a heavy Confederate attack on July 31. Hood now abandoned Atlanta, which was occupied by Sherman on September 1, 1864.

Hood, after several weeks of inactivity, now determined to operate upon Sherman's lengthy line of communications, which stretched four-hundred miles back to Louisville, Kentucky. After substantial maneuvering by both sides throughout most of October, no decisive results had been obtained. Hood's army was still in the field, and Sherman's communications were still secure. Leaving Thomas and Schofield behind to watch Hood, Sherman cut loose from his supply lines on November 15 and

Above: Aerial view of the Franklin battlefield. Dot: Franklin. Left: Union artillery unit "at the ready," for the camera.

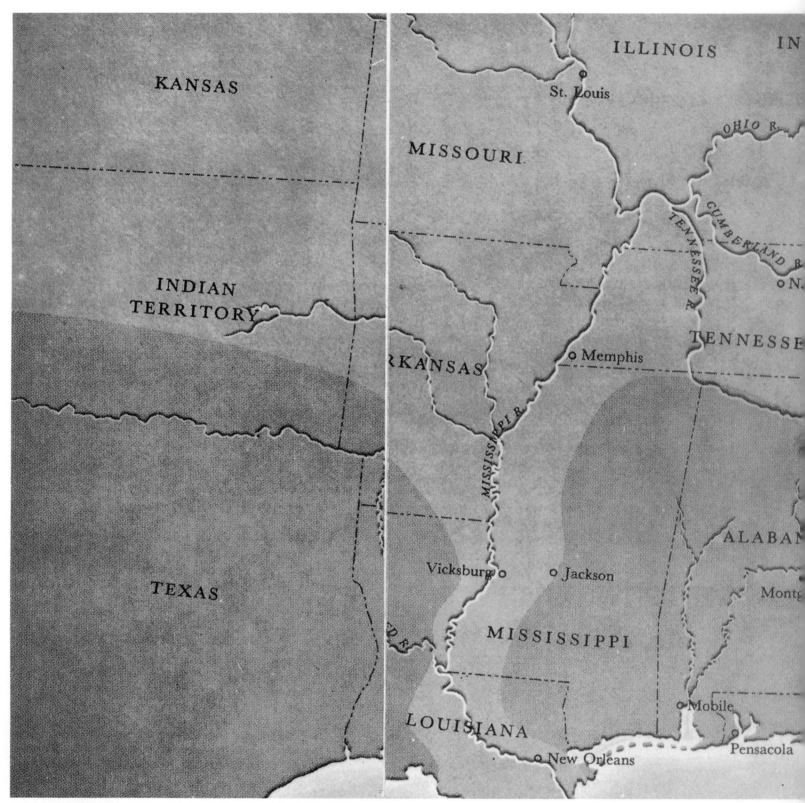

The map shows the 1864 Federal thrusts into the shrinking confederacy; the dotted lines are the ultimate courses of Sherman and Grant.

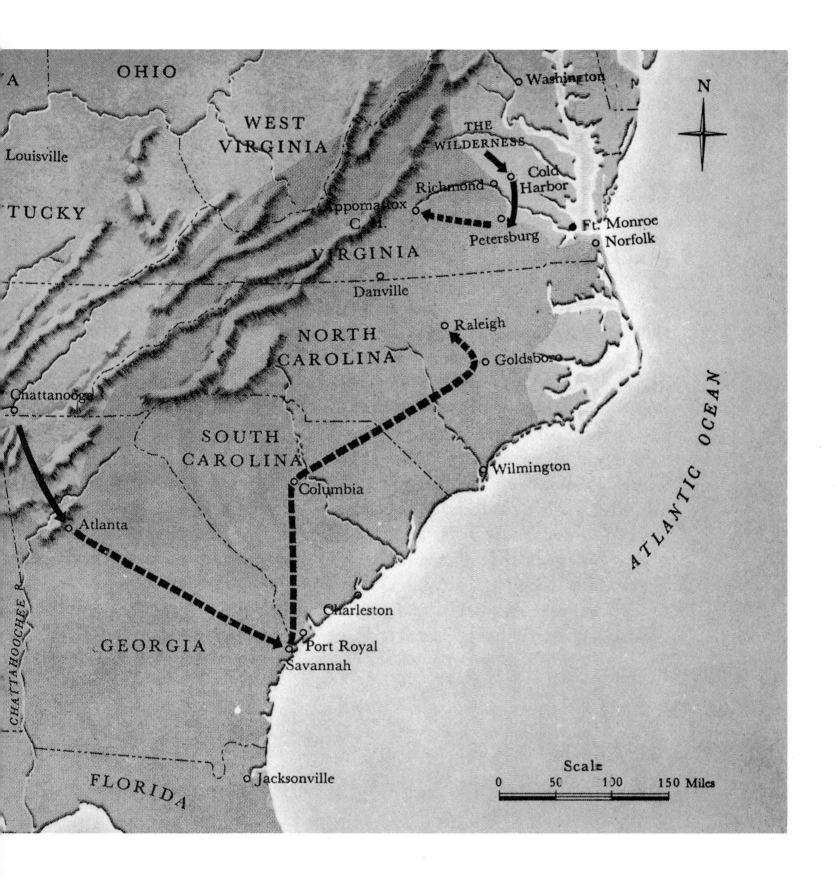

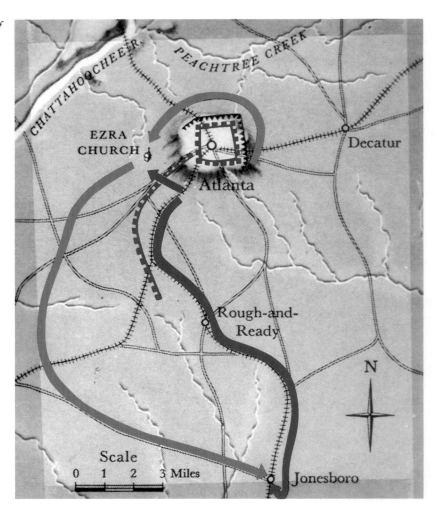

*Right: Sherman's investment of
Atlanta is shown in blue.
The map indicates the
Battle of Ezra Church and
Hood's evacuation of the city.*

*Below: The map shows Hood's July 20
thrust at Peachtree Creek and
his flank attack two days later,
known as the Battle of Atlanta. Blue: Union, Red: Confederate*

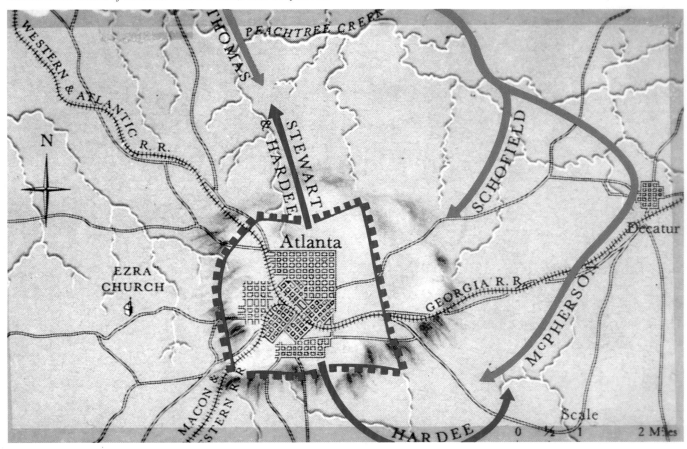

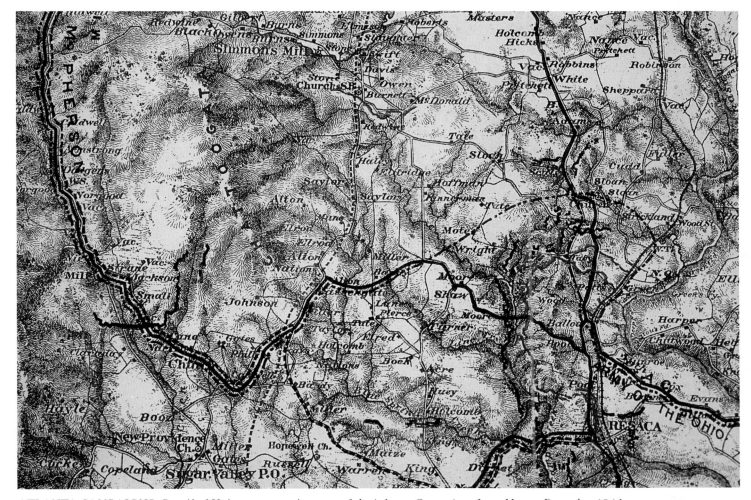

ATLANTA CAMPAIGNS. Detail of Union map, tracing part of the Atlanta Campaigns from May to December 1864.

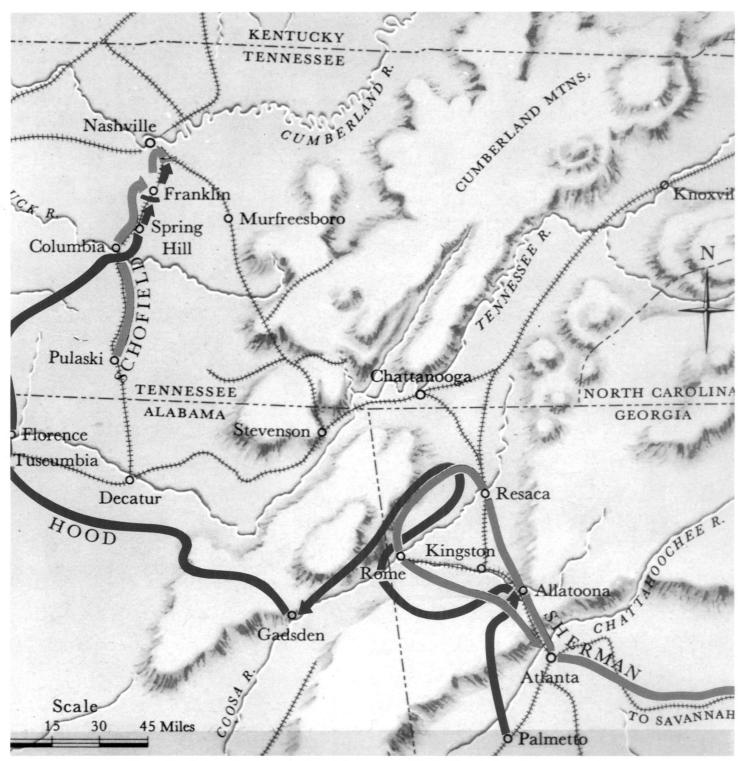

Above: Hood's long, looping route from Atlanta toward Nashville is indicated on the map above.
Blue: Union, Red: Confederate

FRANKLIN: Having escaped the Rebels at Spring Hill, Schofield's army reaches Franklin by noon of November 30. The supply wagons are moved across the Harpeth River (1), as the troops form behind breastworks south of town. Hood approaches two hours later and at 3 P.M. orders the attack (2). This onslaught sweeps the Federal advance back along the Columbia Pike, and the Rebels pour through the Union line near the Gin House (3). At the Carter House (4) General Emerson Opdycke rallies enough Northerners to plug the gap. Further attacks along the Federal line (5) prove fruitless, and the battle sputters out at 9 P.M. That night Schofield pulled his army out of Franklin and joined Thomas' force at Nashville on December 1.

FRANKLIN
November 30, 1864

TO NASHVILLE

FORT GRANGER

Carter's Creek

CARTER HOUSE

Franklin

GIN HOUSE

COLUMBIA PIKE

LEWISBURG PIKE

HARPETH RIVER

NASHVILLE

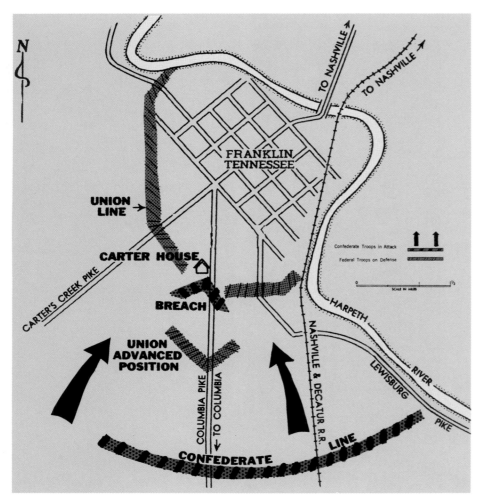

commenced his famous "March to the Sea."

Hood now embarked upon an ambitious plan, designed to disrupt Sherman's intentions by capturing Nashville, Tennessee, and invading Kentucky, causing enough consternation among Union military and political leaders that Sherman would be recalled to deal with Hood's army. The Confederates left northern Alabama on November 22 and were soon joined by Nathan Bedford Forrest's cavalry. Opposing Hood directly was Schofield's XXIII Corps. Schofield's troops, falling back skillfully before Hood's three infantry corps, narrowly averted being cut off at Spring Hill, Tennessee. Hood, angered at the enemy's escape, ordered an assault on their position at Franklin, Tennessee, the following day, November 30. The result was a crushing defeat for the Confederacy, with twelve general officers killed, wounded, or captured.

Schofield retired to the defenses of Nashville, Tennessee, and consolidated his troops with those of Thomas. Hood, though his force was numerically inferior, attempted to invest and lay siege to Nashville. Thomas carefully, and perhaps too cautiously, planned his offensive against Hood for almost two weeks, finally attacking the Confederates on December 15 and routing them in a two-day battle. Hood was ultimately relieved of command. The remnants of his command were sent to North Carolina to oppose Sherman's advance through that state. Making their last attack on their old nemesis at the Battle of Bentonville, North Carolina, on March 19–21, 1865, the remnants of the once-proud Army of Tennessee surrendered with the rest of Johnston's troops at Bennett Place, near Durham, North Carolina, on April 14, 1865.

Top to bottom:
Maj. Gen. William T. Sherman
Maj. Gen. John B. Hood
Gen. Joseph E. Johnston
Maj. Gen. George H. Thomas

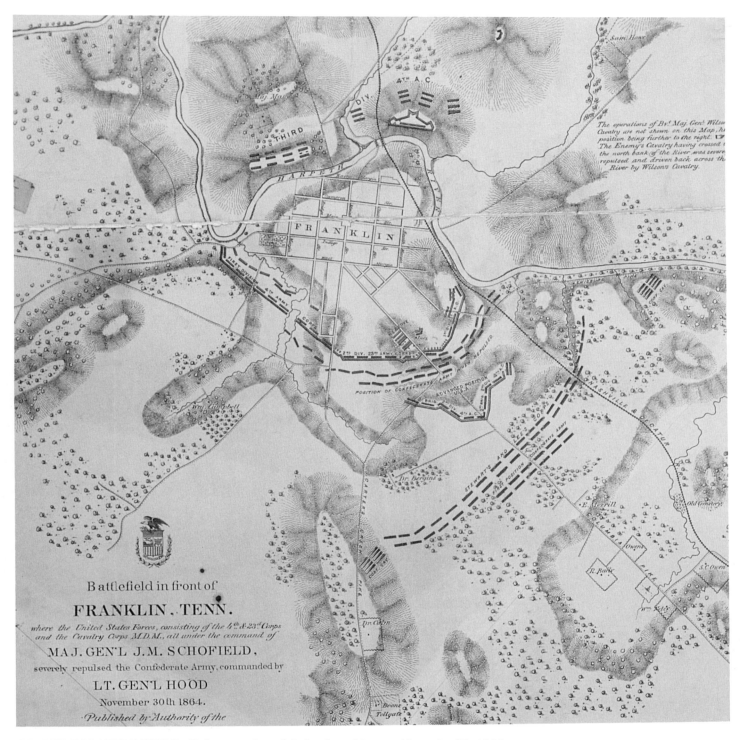

FRANKLIN BATTLEFIELD. *Union overview of the battle positions on November 30, 1864.*

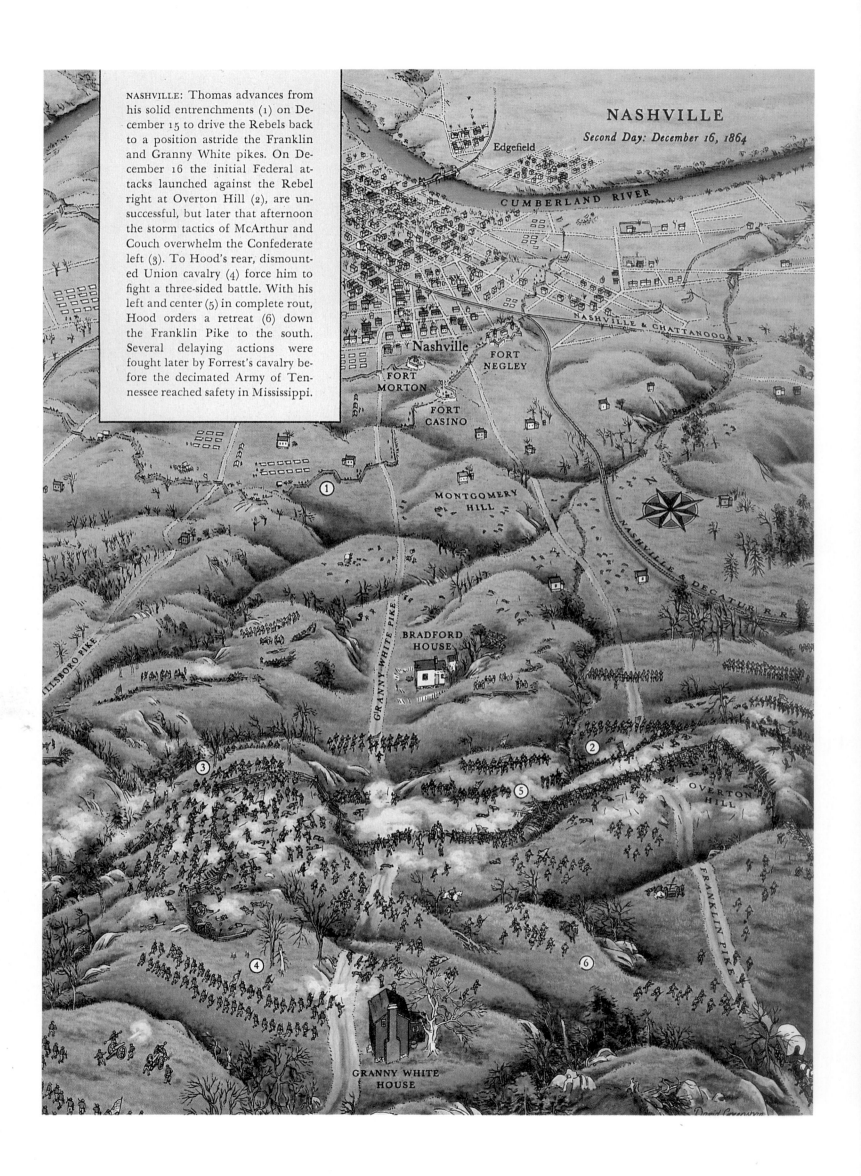

NASHVILLE: Thomas advances from his solid entrenchments (1) on December 15 to drive the Rebels back to a position astride the Franklin and Granny White pikes. On December 16 the initial Federal attacks launched against the Rebel right at Overton Hill (2), are unsuccessful, but later that afternoon the storm tactics of McArthur and Couch overwhelm the Confederate left (3). To Hood's rear, dismounted Union cavalry (4) force him to fight a three-sided battle. With his left and center (5) in complete rout, Hood orders a retreat (6) down the Franklin Pike to the south. Several delaying actions were fought later by Forrest's cavalry before the decimated Army of Tennessee reached safety in Mississippi.

NASHVILLE

Second Day: December 16, 1864

Edgefield

CUMBERLAND RIVER

NASHVILLE & CHATTANOOGA R.R.

Nashville

FORT NEGLEY

FORT MORTON

FORT CASINO

MONTGOMERY HILL

HILLSBORO PIKE

GRANNY WHITE PIKE

BRADFORD HOUSE

NASHVILLE & DECATUR R.R.

OVERTON HILL

FRANKLIN PIKE

GRANNY WHITE HOUSE

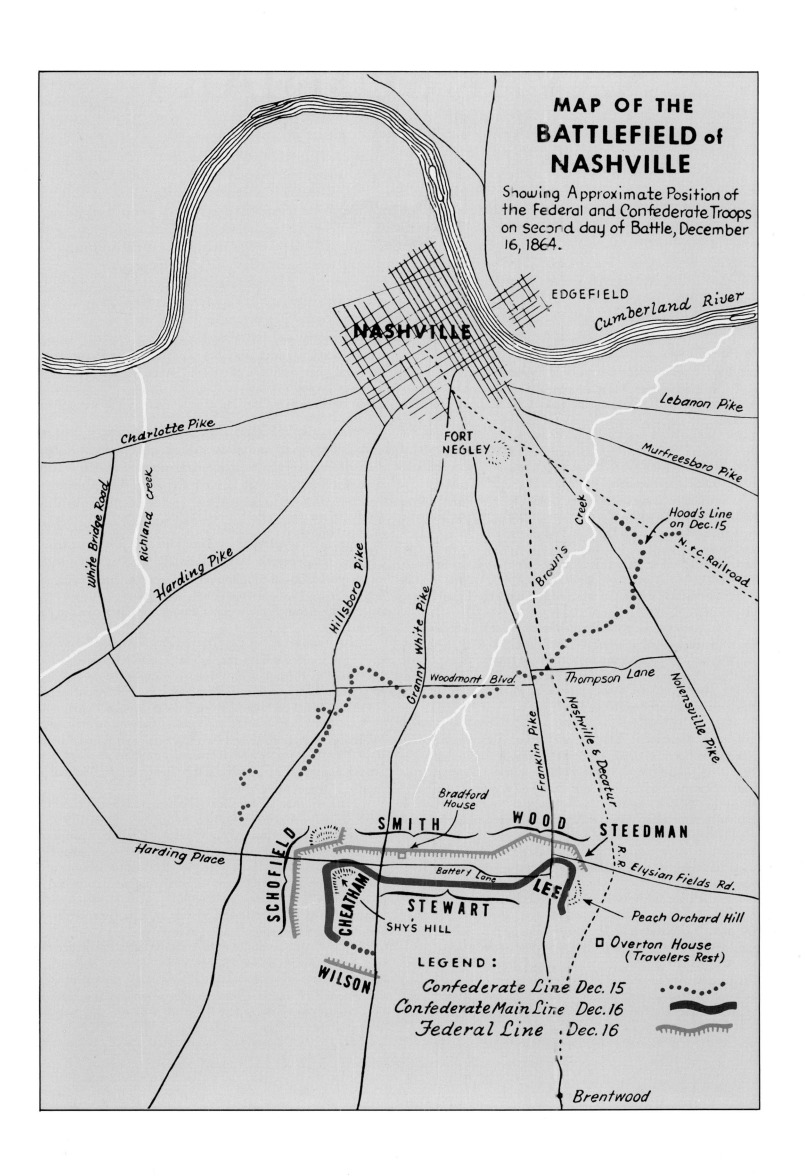

MAP OF THE
BATTLEFIELD of
NASHVILLE

Showing Approximate Position of
the Federal and Confederate Troops
on second day of Battle, December
16, 1864.

EDGEFIELD

Cumberland River

NASHVILLE

Charlotte Pike

Lebanon Pike

Murfreesboro Pike

FORT
NEGLEY

White Bridge Road

Richland Creek

Harding Pike

Hillsboro Pike

Granny White Pike

Brown's Creek

Hood's Line
on Dec.15

N.r.C. Railroad

Woodmont Blvd.

Thompson Lane

Franklin Pike

Nashville & Decatur

Nolensville Pike

Bradford
House

SMITH

WOOD

STEEDMAN

Harding Place

SCHOFIELD

CHEATHAM

Battery Lane

LEE

R.R. Elysian Fields Rd.

STEWART

SHY'S HILL

Peach Orchard Hill

Overton House
(Travelers Rest)

WILSON

LEGEND:
Confederate Line Dec. 15
Confederate Main Line Dec. 16
Federal Line Dec. 16

Brentwood

NAVAL SUMMARY

With the outbreak of the war, the United States navy found itself in the midst of its most important transition of the nineteenth century—the conversion from sail to steam. With a fleet of some ninety vessels, only forty of which were steam-driven, it was unprepared to enforce the blockade declared by President Abraham Lincoln in May of 1861. Its five most powerful warships, steam frigates mounting over forty guns each, were all out of commission, as were many of the other steam vessels.

The Confederate coastline stretched for over 3,500 miles, and in order for the blockade to be recognized by non-belligerent nations, every mile would have to be patrolled, harbors blocked and bases established. The navy department had a formidable task ahead of it. For his first secretary of the navy Lincoln chose Gideon Welles, in part for political reasons, but Welles and his able assistant, Gustavas V. Fox, proved more than equal to the challenge.

The Union certainly had much to be thankful for. Most of the important naval installations, excepting Norfolk, Virginia, and Pensacola, Florida, remained in Union hands. Able officers, such as David G. Farragut, the Porter brothers, David and William, and Samuel du Pont, stood ready to command the fleets the navy would ultimately launch.

On the Confederate side, Jefferson Davis had also picked an able man, Stephen R. Mallory, as his secretary of the navy. Veteran officers of high reputation, among them Franklin Buchanan, Matthew Fontaine Maury, Raphael Semmes and Jodiah Tattnall, had joined the fledgling Confederate navy. What they lacked was ships and, unlike the North, they lacked the industrial base to create them rapidly. With this deficiency readily apparent, the Confederacy sent James D. Bulloch to England to negotiate for the purchase of fast steam frigates to be used in running the blockade—unarmed—because England was a neutral.

Bulloch not only fulfilled this mission, but also undertook to outfit these blockade runners as armed raiders. The cruises of the *Alabama*, *Florida* and *Shenandoah*, among others, bear testimony to his effectiveness in behalf of the Confederacy.

While the Confederacy went abroad for its initial vessels, Welles and Fox instituted a vigorous program of shipbuilding and purchase of suitable private vessels for conversion to blockaders. By the end of 1861, the navy had over 260 ships in commission, including a number of powerful wooden warships. Realizing that coaling stations and other facilities would be necessary to support the blockading fleets, Welles ordered his commanders to begin moving against the Southern coast in the summer of 1861.

The first expedition, commanded by Silas Stringham for the navy and Benjamin Butler for the army, battled successfully against two newly constructed forts guarding the inlets at Cape Hatteras, North Carolina, in August of 1861. By November of that year, the navy was ready to mount a larger and more ambitious assault on Port Royal, South Carolina. Utilizing his ships to neutralize the Confederate forts, du Pont landed some 16,000 army troops to capture Port Royal and Hilton Head, South Carolina. The facilities established there were to play a major role in blockading and amphibious military operations along the Atlantic coast. Two small operations on the Gulf coast, near New Orleans, Louisiana, were successfully carried out before the end of 1861.

By the beginning of 1862, the navy stood ready to support army operations on both the Atlantic and Gulf coasts. From February 8 to the end of April, these joint incursions captured New Bern, Roanoke Island, Elizabeth City and Fort Macon in North Carolina; Fort Pulaski, Brunswick in Georgia; Fernandina, St. Augustine and Jacksonville, as well as Apalachicola, in Florida. Additional operations seized Pass Christian and Biloxi, Mississippi. The stage was now set for two major events: the capture of a major Southern city by naval forces alone and the first trial by combat of the ironclad warship.

Farragut, then a flag officer, was assigned to command the West Gulf Blockading Squadron in January of 1862, with a primary mission of capturing New Orleans. His fleet consisted of four steam sloops and twelve gunboats. Twenty-one schooners converted into mortar boats were placed under the command of David D. Porter. New Orleans's primary defenses consisted of two masonry forts, Jackson and St. Phillip, near the mouth of the Mississippi. A Confederate side-wheeler ram, the *Governor Moore*, and several smaller ships, waited in reserve.

Initial Union attempts by the mortar boats to silence the forts proved unsuccessful. However, two gunboats managed to breach a massive log obstruction placed across the river by the Confederates. Farragut, with the audacity which was to mark all his future operations, ordered the fleet to run the gauntlet between the two forts. The forts, though still formidable, were successfully passed and cut off. A gallant sortie by the *Governor Moore* and escorting craft resulted in the sinking of the U.S.S. *Varuna*, but Farragut's powerful force soon scattered or sank the Southern vessels. New Orleans surrendered and was soon occupied by Union troops under Butler.

With the secession of Virginia in 1861, state authorities had lost little time in seizing the Norfolk, Virginia, navy yard, which had been hastily abandoned by the Union forces on April 20. Among the items left behind, which included one thousand cannon, was the scuttled steam frigate, *Merrimac*. Secretary Mallory saw the potential of this vessel and proposed to raise her and convert the former Union vessel into a Confederate ironclad, to be re-christened C.S.S. *Virginia*. Resourceful Confederate engineers put the ship's engines in working order, and sheared off the top decks, replacing them with a smaller, slanted compartment, housing eleven guns and the pilot house. Two-inch armor on the compartment's sloping sides and a bow ram completed the conversion. The Union authorities, hearing of the work being carried out at Norfolk, hastily planned countermeasures. These took the form of approving a design submitted by John Ericsson, a Swedish naval architect. The *Monitor*, as Ericsson's design came to be called, boasted two eleven-inch inch guns in an armored, revolving turret, with a fully armored deck. Drawing only twelve feet of water, the ship presented the lowest possible profile. Christened on February 25, 1862, the *Monitor* left New York under tow for Hampton Roads, Virginia. The departure was not a moment too soon; the *Virginia* had been christened eight days before.

On the morning of March 8, the *Virginia*, under command of Franklin Buchanan, steamed into Hampton Roads with the mission of breaking the Union blockade at that point. Attacking and rapidly sinking the U.S.S. *Cumberland* (32 guns) and the *Congress* (52 guns), Buchanan turned on the steam frigate, *Minnesota*, and chased her aground. The Confederates, justly elated with their success, returned to port, intending to finish off the *Minnesota* and the rest of the Union blockading fleet the next day. When the *Virginia* steamed into Hampton Roads the next morning, the *Monitor*, having arrived the night before, was waiting. For over four hours, the two ships pounded each other to little advantage. Yet the *Monitor* had preserved the Union blockade and her design spawned dozens of similar vessels. The Confederates were eventually forced to abandon Norfolk, destroying the *Virginia* during the evacuation. The brief career of the *Monitor* ended on December 31, 1862, sunk in a gale off the North Carolina coast.

For the remainder of 1862, the U.S. navy continued to solidify its hold on the Confederate coast. The naval yard at Pensacola, Florida, was recaptured in May, and Galveston, Texas, was regained in October. On the Mississippi River, forces under Farragut and David D. Porter captured Baton Rouge, Louisiana, subdued Island Number10 and occupied Memphis, Tennessee, after a spirited engagement with a vastly inferior Southern naval force. By the end of the year, only Port Hudson, Louisiana, and Vicksburg, Mississippi, remained in Confederate hands.

Anxious to answer requests from Washington for further action, Farragut undertook in June of 1862 to run past the batteries at Vicksburg, hoping to damage them substantially with naval gunfire. Eight of his eleven ships successfully passed the Confederate citadel, but Farragut was convinced that naval action alone would not be effective against Vicksburg. On July 15, the Confederates attacked part of the Union fleet near Vicksburg with the newly built ram, C.S.S. *Arkansas*. Farragut, with the main body of his fleet, again fought his way past the Vicksburg batteries and also dueled the *Arkansas* in an inconclusive action. Farragut then returned to New Orleans until March of 1863, when the navy began operations to assist U. S. Grant's final campaign for Vicksburg. In this the navy provided transport-escort services and some support from Porter's gunboat flotilla. With the fall of Vicksburg on July 4, 1863, and the surrender of Port Hudson, Louisiana, soon thereafter, the Mississippi River was now under Union control.

Despite the number of Union ships participating in the blockade and the positions occupied on the Confederate shoreline, the blockade runners were still successfully penetrating the naval cordon. With Wilmington, North Carolina, Charleston, South Carolina, and Mobile, Alabama, still in Southern hands, the odds were still in favor of the audacious blockade runners. A campaign was launched by du Pont, using a number of "monitors," to reduce Fort Sumter in Charleston harbor. In a day-long battle on April 7, 1863, du Pont attempted to silence the fort. Once again, it was demonstrated that naval forces alone could not silence coastal forts. Charleston remained in Confederate hands until captured in a land battle in February of 1865.

In the summer of 1864, forces under Farragut were assembled for an attack on Mobile, Alabama, the last major point on the Gulf coast still in Southern hands. On August 5, 1864, Farragut's fleet of fourteen wooden ships and four monitors steamed into Mobile Bay. The Confederates were well-prepared, boasting a fort, submerged pilings, buoyed mines and a powerful ironclad, the C.S.S. *Tennessee*. As Farragut's attacking force, led by the *Brooklyn* and followed by his flagship, *Hartford*, approached the defenses, the monitor, *Tecumseh*, eager to close with the *Tennessee*, steamed ahead. Striking a submerged mine or torpedo, the *Tecumseh* sank almost immediately, with a loss of eighty-per cent of her crew. The *Brooklyn*, first in line, feared a similar fate and stopped engines. Farragut, lashed to the rigging of the *Hartford*, exploded with his oft-quoted "Damn the torpedoes! Full steam ahead." After a four-hour battle with Buchanan's *Tennessee*, the Union fleet overwhelmed the Confederate ironclad and seized control of Mobile Bay. Though the city and its forts did not surrender until April of 1865, the port was effectively closed to blockade runners.

With Charleston heavily besieged and Mobile Bay closed, Wilmington, North Carolina, became the Confederacy's last important port that could handle the vital blockade runners. Protected by Fort Fisher and an extensive earthen fort, Wilmington appeared impregnable. The job of capturing the last Southern sea bastion fell to David D. Porter. Assembling a powerful fleet based in Hampton Roads, Porter was to support an army expedition led by Butler. The first attack, in December of 1864, ended in failure when Butler refused to assault the fort. Butler was replaced by Alfred H. Terry. In a fierce three-day battle, January 12–15, 1865, Porter and Terry succeeded in capturing Fort Fisher. The Union navy had effectively ended blockade-running operations into the Confederacy.

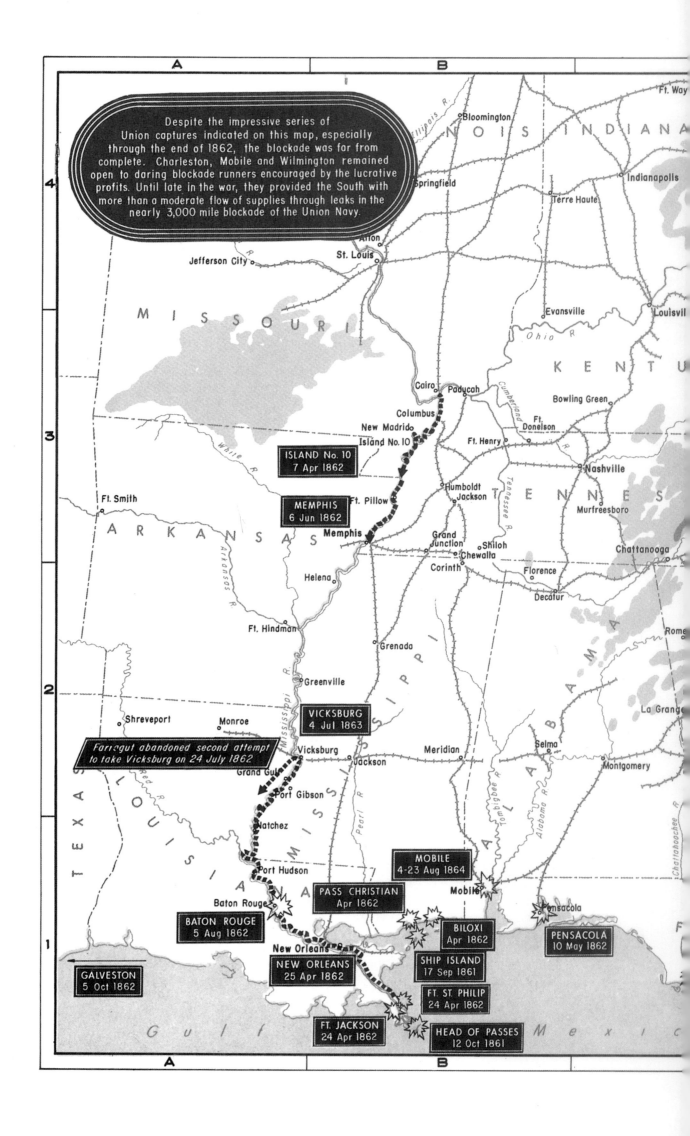

Despite the impressive series of Union captures indicated on this map, especially through the end of 1862, the blockade was far from complete. Charleston, Mobile and Wilmington remained open to daring blockade runners encouraged by the lucrative profits. Until late in the war, they provided the South with more than a moderate flow of supplies through leaks in the nearly 3,000 mile blockade of the Union Navy.

ISLAND No. 10
7 Apr 1862

MEMPHIS
6 Jun 1862

VICKSBURG
4 Jul 1863

Farragut abandoned second attempt
to take Vicksburg on 24 July 1862

MOBILE
4-23 Aug 1864

PASS CHRISTIAN
Apr 1862

BILOXI
Apr 1862

PENSACOLA
10 May 1862

BATON ROUGE
5 Aug 1862

SHIP ISLAND
17 Sep 1861

NEW ORLEANS
25 Apr 1862

GALVESTON
5 Oct 1862

FT. ST. PHILIP
24 Apr 1862

FT. JACKSON
24 Apr 1862

HEAD OF PASSES
12 Oct 1861

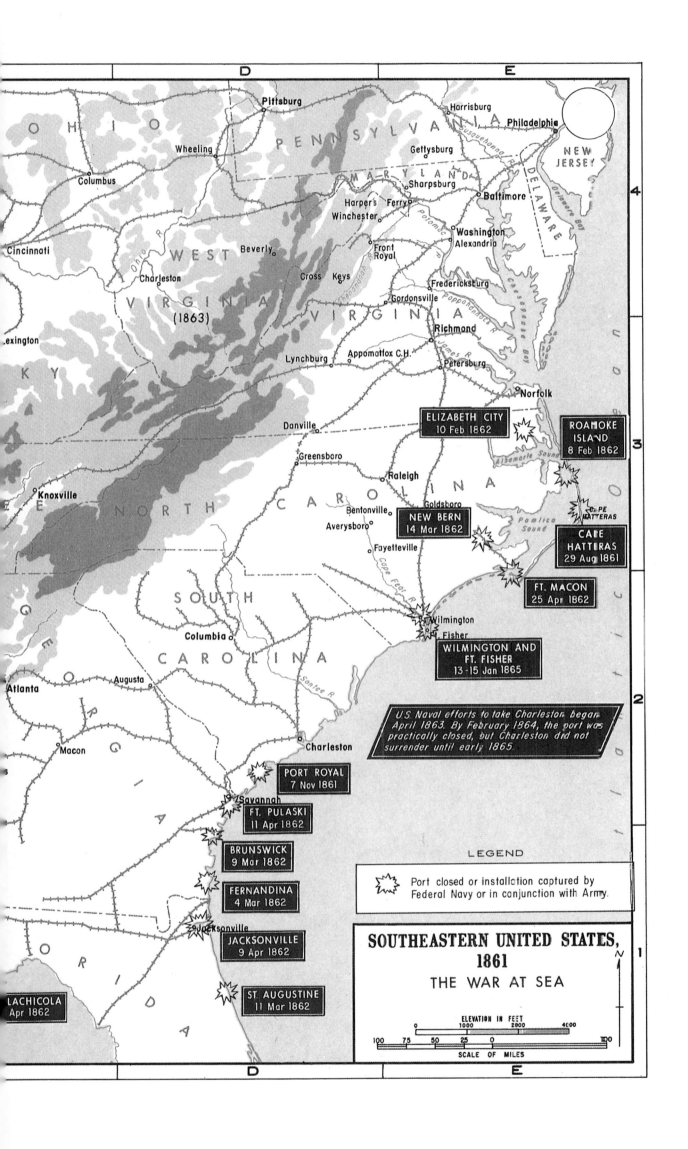

OHIO

Columbus

Cincinnati

Lexington

KENTUCKY

Knoxville

PENNSYLVANIA
Pittsburg

Wheeling

Harrisburg
Philadelphia

NEW JERSEY

Gettysburg

WEST VIRGINIA (1863)
Charleston
Beverly

Columbus

MARYLAND
Sharpsburg

Harper's Ferry
Winchester

Baltimore

Washington
Alexandria

DELAWARE

Delaware Bay

Front Royal

Cross Keys

VIRGINIA

Fredericksburg

Gordonsville

Lynchburg

Appomattox C.H.

Richmond

Petersburg

James R.

Norfolk

Danville

Greensboro

Raleigh

NORTH CAROLINA

Goldsboro

Bentonville

Averysboro

Fayetteville

Cape Fear R.

Chesapeake Bay

ELIZABETH CITY
10 Feb 1862

ROANOKE ISLAND
8 Feb 1862

Albemarle Sound

CAPE HATTERAS

NEW BERN
14 Mar 1862

Pamlico Sound

CAPE HATTERAS
29 Aug 1861

FT. MACON
25 Apr 1862

Wilmington
Fisher

WILMINGTON AND FT. FISHER
13-15 Jan 1865

SOUTH CAROLINA

Columbia

Santee R.

Atlanta

Augusta

U.S. Naval efforts to take Charleston began April 1863. By February 1864, the port was practically closed, but Charleston did not surrender until early 1865.

GEORGIA

Macon

Charleston

PORT ROYAL
7 Nov 1861

Savannah

FT. PULASKI
11 Apr 1862

BRUNSWICK
9 Mar 1862

FERNANDINA
4 Mar 1862

Jacksonville

JACKSONVILLE
9 Apr 1862

FLORIDA

LACHICOLA
Apr 1862

ST. AUGUSTINE
11 Mar 1862

LEGEND

Port closed or installation captured by Federal Navy or in conjunction with Army.

SOUTHEASTERN UNITED STATES, 1861
THE WAR AT SEA

N

ELEVATION IN FEET
1000   2000   4000

100   75   50   25   0   100

SCALE OF MILES

Sails augmented steam in the U.S.S. Pensacola, *pride of the prewar Union fleet.*

The U.S.S. Cairo, *part of the Federal Fleet at the Battle of Memphis.*

The submarine torpedo boat H. L. Huntley *in a painting by Conrad Wise Chapman, December 6, 1963.*

Naval ordinance of the Civil War era was highly effective against wooden ships. Only ironclads could stand up to such firepower in ship-to-ship duels. The Parrott rifle threw a 100-pound shell with reasonable accuracy for one mile.

EIGHT GENERALS

GEORGE GORDON MEADE (1815–72)

West Point class of 1835. He resigned from the army the follow-ing year to take up a career in civil engineering, but in 1842 he rejoined the military to serve as a civil engineer and surveyor. A captain when war broke out, Meade was appointed brigadier general of Pennsylvania volunteers by the state governor. In 1862, after organizing the defenses of Washington, D.C., he was severely wounded twice in the Seven Days' battles. On recovery, he commanded a corps in the Army of the Potomac under Joseph Hooker at Chancellorsville. This disastrous battle led President Abraham Lincoln to replace Hooker with Meade on June 28, 1863, promoting him over others more senior, who willingly served under him—a tribute to him as a talented, hardworking, truly professional soldier.

After only three days of his new command, the Battle of Gettysburg began, almost by accident. Against Meade was the fact that successive Union defeats had persuaded many of the soldiers that Robert E. Lee was invincible; in Meade's favor, the South was no longer fighting on its own territory. Pennsylvanians were delighted to see Union forces in pursuit of the enemy, and cheered them on their way, providing some much-needed moral boosting as well as food. The three days of battle were marked by carnage, heroism, and errors on the part of subordinates. Meade's outstanding command abilities carried the field, how-ever, and the only criticism he faced was the one of failing to pursue the retreating enemy (he allowed his exhausted men some rest and attended to the wounded and prisoners—as Lee had known he would). At Gettysburg, Meade achieved what his predecessors could not—the decisive victory of the war.

When U. S. Grant was appointed general-in-chief, and made his headquarters with Meade's Army of the Potomac, Meade, in effect, became his subordinate in subsequent battles. He was rewarded with the rank of major general in August 1864, on Grant's recommendation, and remained in the army after war's end. He was in command of the military Division of the Atlantic at the time of his death of pneumonia in 1872.

AMBROSE POWELL HILL (1825–65)

West Point class of 1847. A veteran of the Mexican War and a variety of other duties, Hill resigned from the army in March 1861 to serve as colonel in the Virginia infantry, receiving a promotion to brigadier general in February 1862. Only three months later, after the Peninsular Campaign, he became major general, the youngest in the Army of Northern Virginia, and, according to Robert E. Lee, "the best soldier of his grade with me." Stonewall Jackson, however, under whom Hill served, did not agree, and relations between the two were far from cordial. Matters reached a point where Jackson was demanding outright dismissal of the commander of the strongest and best division of the army, whose successes had aided Jackson's own victories substantially.

After Jackson's wounding at Chancellorsville, Hill briefly took command, but he was forced to relinquish it almost immediately to Jeb Stuart after being painfully wounded in the legs. With his promotion to lieutenant general in May 1863, he took command of the newly formed III Corps. Admired by his men as well as by his staff officers, he was an excellent administrator, but he was beginning to lose his flair and brilliance. It is thought that his lapses in personality were due to psychosomatic ailments, or even to fear of his great responsibilities. His earlier triumphant performances during the Seven Days' battles, Cedar Mountain and Antietam were not to be duplicated.

Tragically, Hill was killed by a Union straggler on the lines at Petersburg on April 2, 1865—only a week before General Lee's surrender at Appomattox Courthouse, Virginia.

JOSEPH HOOKER (1814–79)

West Point class of 1837. While serving as a staff officer in the Mexican War, Hooker distinguished himself for "gallant and meritorious conduct" and was brevetted lieutenant colonel. He became assistant adjutant general of the Pacific Division, resigned from the army in 1853, and took up farming in California. In 1861, he was commissioned brigadier general of volunteers. During the Peninsular Campaign of May 1862, in which his troops were in the forefront of the fighting, he received the nickname "Fighting Joe," for his bravery and determination under fire. In command of a corps at Antietam, he was severely wounded and had to be carried from the battlefield, subsequently being named brigadier general in the regular army.

Ambrose Burnside's defeat at Fredericksburg gave rise to criticism by his subordinates (Hooker among them) of his conduct of the battle. When Burnside demanded their removal, President Abraham Lincoln instead accepted Burnside's resignation and named Hooker commander of the Army of the Potomac. Hooker set about reorganizing and reforming his forces. Aided by the intelligence system he had set up, his plan for the Battle of Chancellorsville was both sound and creative—but his overconfidence in his own judgment, and then his indecisiveness, lost the day for the Union, despite the fact that his troops outnumbered Robert E. Lee's by more than two to one. On June 28, 1863, he asked to be relieved of his command after being refused reinforcements, and George G. Meade took his place. He then became a corps commander under William T. Sherman, whom he served well. Insulted at being passed over for command of the Army of the Tennessee, he left field service. Later, he commanded several departments of the army, resigning with the rank of major general in 1868.

Hooker's personal characteristics have received almost as much attention from biographers as his military strengths and weaknesses. Although friends and colleagues close to him denied it, it was widely believed that he overindulged in both drink and women—in fact, the army's camp followers were derisively known as "hookers." Even worse, his headquarters was described as a place where "no gentleman cared to go and no lady could go."

WILLIAM TECUMSEH SHERMAN (1820–91)

West Point class of 1840. He resigned his army commission in 1853, eventually becoming superintendent of a military academy in Pineville, Louisiana (now Louisiana State University). Successful and popular, he was offered a high rank in the Confederate army, but after Louisiana's secession he left the state in May 1861, and was appointed colonel in command of a division of Union volunteers. He fought valiantly at Shiloh, earning promotion to major general. In command of a corps of the Army of the Tennessee under Grant, he took part in the amphibious campaign at Vicksburg. When the city fell, he was appointed brigadier general in the regular army in recognition of his distinguished service.

In October 1863, he was made commander of the Army of the Tennessee; by March 1864, with U. S. Grant's departure, he commanded the three Union armies in the west, with orders to advance against Atlanta. After a six-week siege, John B. Hood abandoned the city. Sherman ordered the evacuation of all civilians and the destruction of any installations of military value. By now a major general, he began his twenty-four-day march to the sea. Despite orders to the contrary, soldiers and stragglers cut a terrible path of desolation through the countryside. Sherman later maintained that there was no violence toward noncombatants, and that it was far better to end the war quickly by destroying supplies and lines of communication than to endure further bloodshed. From Savannah, Georgia, Sherman marched north through the Carolinas, meeting no effective resistance, and finally accepted Joseph E. Johnston's surrender near Durham, North Carolina, on April 26, 1865, seventeen days after Lee's capitulation at Appomattox.

Sherman remained in the army after the war, becoming its commander-in-chief on U.S. Grant's taking office as President. He established the army training school at Fort Leavenworth, Kansas, a lasting achievement, and retired in 1883. He forcefully declined the Republican presidential nomination in 1884, preferring to lead an active and productive life in New York City, where he was much in demand at both military and social occasions. His famous statement, "War is hell," was not the remark of a cynic; he believed the war had to be ended by the simplest means, and that peace and union should be restored without draconian punishment—an unpopular view after President Abraham Lincoln's assassination. Many authorities consider him one of the best of the Civil War generals.

ULYSSES SIMPSON GRANT (1822–85)

West Point class of 1843. Grant ranked twenty-first in a class of thirty-nine. A distinguished veteran of the Mexican War, Grant resigned his commission in 1854, perhaps because of differences with his commanding officer over his frequent drinking bouts. Over the next six years, he tried various careers without success, finally working for his brothers as a clerk in their leather shop in Galena, Illinois. At the outbreak of the Civil War, the best he could manage was an appointment as colonel of the 21st Illinois Volunteers. After significant victories in early 1862—the capture of Forts Henry and Donelson, and his avoidance of a near calamitous defeat at Shiloh—he became hugely popular and received the nickname, "Unconditional Surrender."

For the next year, Grant concentrated on the strategically vital Mississippi River port of Vicksburg. After repeated assaults, he besieged the city and finally forced its surrender on July 4, 1863—an impressive victory that gave the North control of the Mississippi and deprived the South of east–west rail as well as river transport. Some nine-hundred miles away, the Battle of Gettysburg was being won by the Union the same day.

Promoted to major general in the regular army, Grant was soon named supreme commander in the west and created lieutenant general, a grade revived especially for him by a grateful Congress.

After a decisive victory at Chattanooga, President Abraham Lincoln named him commander–in–chief of the Union armies. Grant elected to make his headquarters with the Army of the Potomac, which was under the command of George G. Meade. For the next year, Grant directed the union forces in costly and often indecisive battles—the Wilderness, Spotsylvania, Cold Harbor—for a total loss of 60,000 men by early summer 1864. This policy of attrition, though bloody, eventually forced Lee to move his forces westward for a greater degree of safety and maneuverability, but he was run to ground at Appomattox and had to surrender on April 9, 1865. The war was virtually over.

In 1866, Congress conferred the title of full general on Grant, making him the first officer to hold this rank since the Revolutionary War.

Nominated by the Republican party in 1868, he served two terms as president. Although his personal honesty was never questioned, his administrations were infamous for their corruption, graft, and bitter factionalism. Once out of office, Grant found himself again burdened with the cycle of poverty, failure, and debt, until he began receiving an army pension as a retired general. His memoirs, barely finished before his death, earned the then unprecedented sum of over $400,000 for his family.

THOMAS JONATHAN "STONEWALL" JACKSON (1824–63)

West Point class of 1846 (the class that was to provide no fewer than twenty-four general officers on both sides of the conflict). Jackson reached the rank of brevet major in the Mexican War, resigning from the army in 1852 after becoming an instructor at the Virginia Military Institute. An unsung colonel of the Virginia militia in command at Harpers Ferry, he was promoted to brigadier general in the Confederate army by June 1861. In July of that year, Barnard Bee described him as "standing like a stone wall" at the First Battle of Bull Run, and the description endured.

On the whole, Jackson's Shenandoah Valley Campaign of 1862 was a complete success. Jackson was the hero of the South, going on to victory after victory—notably at Cedar Mountain and Second Bull Run. In 1862, Robert E. Lee promoted him to lieutenant general and put him in charge of II Corps. His success continued with the battles of Fredericksburg and Chancellorsville. It was at Chancellorsville that Jackson was wounded by his own troops on May 2, dying of pneumonia eight days later after the amputation of his left arm. On hearing of this, Lee said, "He has lost his left arm, but I have lost my right arm."

It is undeniably true that Jackson was one of Lee's most brilliant generals. His concern for his men (like Lee's) made them willing to perform nearly impossible feats; his troops maneuvered so swiftly on the battlefield that they became known as "foot cavalry." His tactical genius perfectly complemented Lee's overall strategic designs. Together they seemed invincible. Had Jackson lived, the outcome of the war might have been the same, but its course would arguably have been much different.

JAMES LONGSTREET (1821–1904)

West Point class of 1842. Longstreet was cited for gallantry in the Mexican War and reached the rank of major in the army before resigning in June, 1861. Sixteen days later, he was appointed brigadier general in the Confederate army. By October of that year, he was made a major general after threatening to resign because newly joined officers were being promoted over him. Personal tragedy struck in January 1862, when three of his children died as a result of a scarlet fever epidemic in Richmond.

He subsequently distinguished himself in the Peninsular Campaign and at Second Bull Run and Sharpsburg. As lieutenant general, the senior man holding that rank, he held an impregnable position at Fredericksburg, where his artillery delivered devastating fire upon wave after wave of attacking Union forces. In command of the right wing at Gettysburg, he was unfairly charged with losing the battle for the South because of his delay in attacking the Union position.

Seriously wounded in the Battle of the Wilderness on May 6, 1864, Longstreet took months to recover. During the final period of the war, he took command of his troops—arranging, as a friend of Grant's from before the war, the details of Lee's surrender at Appomattox. Longstreet was the only one of his rank to surrender with the men under his command, typical of an officer who had always merited the respect of his troops, to whom he was known as "Old Pete." Considered the best battlefield tactician either side could boast (Lee affectionately called him "my old War Horse"), he was far less successful as an independent commander.

After the war, Longstreet became harshly critical of Lee's strategy at Gettysburg. On settling in New Orleans, he joined the Republican party. His criticisms of Lee, and his acceptance of Washington appointments (minister to Turkey in 1880, Pacific railroads commissioner from 1897 to 1904) made him highly unpopular in the South. He died at eighty-three, the last of the Confederate generals.

INDEX

ROBERT EDWARD LEE (1807–70)

West Point Class of 1829 (in which he ranked second). After seventeen years of engineering work, Lee found in the outbreak of the Mexican War the opportunity to prove his superior leadership abilities. Then he was commandant of West Point from 1852 to 1855, serving in Texas when the Civil War broke out. Neither pro-slavery nor secessionist, he still refused President Abraham Lincoln's offer of command of the Union forces, and when Virginia seceded, he resigned his commission. In June 1861, he was confirmed a general of the Confederate States army and became military adviser to President Jefferson Davis. When Joseph E. Johnston was wounded at Seven Pines, Lee took command of the Army of Northern Virginia, promptly foiling a threat against Richmond and defeating the North at Second Bull Run. Then came the victory at Fredericksburg, where he damaged Union morale by his overwhelming defeat of Ambrose Burnside's army in December 1862.

Lee's army was often outnumbered by more than three to one in the field; arms, food, and clothing were low, and his troops' morale was eroded by hunger and exhaustion. At Chancellorsville in May 1863, an early assault by Stonewall Jackson led to a Union rout when Joseph Hooker mistakenly ordered a full retreat. Confederate forces were once again victorious—but at the cost of Jackson's life and other heavy casualties.

A scant two months later, the Battle of Gettysburg would demonstrate the leadership vacuum caused by the deaths not only of Jackson, but of other capable field officers and veteran fighting men. "The price of victory at Chancellorsville was defeat at Gettysburg," wrote one historian. The Army of the Potomac was now on the offensive, and all Lee's efforts and genius could not prevail.

After the war, Lee became president of what was then Washington College in Lexington, Virginia (renamed Washington and Lee University in 1871). Lee spent his remaining years working for the restoration of union and harmony between the former enemies. Even before he died he was a much-admired, almost legendary figure. His gallantry in war and his generosity of spirit still keep their hold on the American heart and mind.

ACKNOWLEDGEMENTS

There are a few people who deserve thanks for making this book possible. First of these is my wife Stella. Many times she urged me to find a publisher for this book, and then remained calm during the five years it took to complete my efforts. Secondly, I want to thank Stephen Rowe for his numerous suggestions on the text as well as his fact-checking of historical and bibliographic details and for the various maps, photographs and research texts he made available to me. Others who have made this book possible are noted artist Don Troiani, many of whose splendid paintings grace the pages of this book and Don Stivers whose picture, *Council of War*, dominates the title pages. Others who have made the path of this book easier and more interesting are the National High Altitude Photography Program, a section of the U.S. Department of the Interior Geological Survey, The Earth Observation Satellite Co., Paul Pugliese and his work on the strategic maps. I am especially indebted for the maps created at West Point to supplement the course in The History of the Military Art. These maps first appeared in 1959 in the unique, two-volume *West Point Atlas of American Wars*. Subsequently, they were modified in *Atlas for the American Civil War*, published by the Avery Publishing Group. For his cordial and expert guidance through the rare, antique maps, Chief, Special Collections, U.S. Military Academy Library, West Point, I am deeply indebted to Alan Aimone. And, lastly, I am thankful for the creative insights of Norman Holt. Their help has been invaluable to the completion of my work.

ILLUSTRATION CREDITS

American Heritage, a division of Forbes Inc., *The American Heritage Picture History of the Civil War:* 12-13, 18-19, 26-27, 34-35, 44, 46, 47 top, 52-53, 55 right, 60-61, 70-71, 78-79, 86-87, 96-97, 105 bottom, 106-107, 116-117, 126-127, 134-135, 144-145, 146 both, 148, 149, 152.

Avery Publishing Group, *The Atlas for the American Civil War*, Thomas E. Griess Series Editor: 10-11, 14, 15, 31, 38-39, 45 top, 64-65, 90-91, 100-101, 110-111, 120-121, 138-139, 156-157.

Confederate Museum: 159 top.

Kunhardt Collection: 16, 24, 50, 58, 68, 84, 132, 142.

Library of Congress: 2, 136, 158 top, 159 bottom, and all portraits on pages 20-21, 29, 37, 45, 47, 54, 62-63, 72, 81, 89, 99, 108-109, 119, 128, 150, 160, 161, 162, 163, 164, 165, 167.

National Archives: 158 bottom.

National Park Service Historical Survey Series: 20-21 top, 28, 36, 54-55 top, 62-63 top, 73, 80, 88, 98-99, 109, 118, 128-129 bottom, 137, 150 top left.

Don Stivers: 6.

Don Troiani: 32, 42, 76, 94, 104, 114, 124.

U.S. National High Altitude Photography Program: 17, 25, 33, 43, 47 bottom left, 51, 59, 69, 77, 85, 95, 105 top right, 115, 125, 133, 143.

Valentine Museum: 166.

West Point Academy Special Collection: 22-23, 30, 40-41, 48-49, 56-57, 66-67, 74-75, 82-83, 92-93, 102-103, 112-113, 122, 123, 130-131, 140-141, 147, 151, 153.